$20.00

NORTH HIGH SCHOOL
MEDIA CENTER
2222 MICHIGAN AVENUE
WAUKESHA, WI 53188

L earning
to Question
to Wonder
to Learn

by Jamie McKenzie

D0066968

FNO Press
500 15th Street
Bellingham, Washington
http://fnopress.com
http://store.yahoo.com/fnopress/
360-647-8759 (Voice and Fax)

FNO Press http://fnopress.com

This work contains some articles previously published in a number of journals and publications.

Chapter One, "Why Question?" first appeared in the November, 2004 issue of **The Question Mark** , Vol 1|No 3|November|2004.

Chapter Two, "Why Wonder?" first appeared in the January, 2005 issue of **The Question Mark,** Vol 1|No 4|January|2005.

Chapter Three, "Questions as Technology," first appeared in **ORBIT** , Vol. 32 , No. 4 , 2002.

Chapter Five, "Quality Teaching" first appeared in the September, 2004 issue of **The Question Mark,** Vol 1|No 2|September|2004.

Copyright © 2005 by Jamieson McKenzie and FNO Press. All rights reserved. No part of this publication may be reproduced or transmitted in any form or by any means, electronic or mechanical, including photocopy, recording or any information storage and retrieval system without express permission from FNO Press at mckenzie@fno.org. Copyright formally registered with the U.S. Office of Copyright.

Learning to Question to Wonder to Learn

is dedicated to Frances McKenzie, my
father's loving younger sister, who
nurtured the questioning, wondering
and dreaming of children as a
teacher in the Newton Schools for
many years and set a fine example
of how one might combine the
art, the science, the craft and the
magic of teaching.

is also dedicated to Jack Nelson, an
inspiring and demanding professor of
social studies education at Rutgers who
more than any other teacher I met during
my years of graduate study encouraged
me to focus my efforts on questioning
and wonder. His faith, encouragement
and high standards had a major impact on
my thinking and my development as a
writer and thinker.

About the author . . .

Jamie McKenzie is the editor of three online journals, **The Question Mark** (http://questioning.org). **From Now On - The Educational Technology Journal** (http://fno.org) and **No Child Left** (http://nochildleft.com).

A graduate of Yale with an M.A. from Columbia and Ed.D. from Rutgers, Jamie has been a middle school teacher of English and social studies, an assistant principal, an elementary principal, an assistant superintendent in Princeton (NJ), and a superintendent of two districts on the East Coast of the States. He also taught four-year-olds in Sunday school.

Jamie has published and spoken extensively on the introduction of new technologies to schools. In recent times, he has paid particular attention to what he calls discerning uses of new technologies.

From 1993-1997, Jamie was the Director of Libraries, Media and Technology for the Bellingham (WA) Public Schools, a district of 19 schools and 10,000 students that was fully networked with 2000 desktops all tied to the Internet in 1995.

Jamie now works with schools and teachers around the world to strengthen the questioning and thinking skills of students.

Late in his career, Jamie has also devoted himself to articulating a case against the damage he sees being done to schools and students by the ill-considered, untested, punitive measures that are part and parcel of NCLB - which he has renamed Helter-Skelter. He argues against fast food education and factory approaches to school improvement, suggesting instead that students be shown how to to think, solve problems and make up their own minds.

A full resume listing publication credits and a detailed career history is available online at http://fno.org/JM/resume.html.

Introduction

Thinking is back in fashion . . . in some countries. Not in others.

Yet it may be that thinking is not enough. We have devoted decades - maybe even centuries - to showing students how to think, but many of those efforts have been wrong-minded and inconsequential. All in all, they have simply been what Pink Floyd called "another brick in the wall."

This book maintains that questioning and wondering are more potent ways of developing understanding than what usually passes for thinking in school programs.

Sadly, thinking does not always lead to understanding or wisdom.

Thinking can be deficient, limited and delusional. It can skirt the real issues and avoid the dark (but promising) side of life. It can be critical rather than creative.

"If you don't eat your meat, you can't have any pudding."

Pink Floyd

Those who think about serious issues and challenges may ask the wrong questions and be captive of biases, wishes, preconceptions and "gut" instincts.

Schools have taught thinking off and on throughout most of the previous century as the fashions dictated, but they have done less well with questioning and wondering.

Schools have done better with critical thinking than creative thinking, but one can hardly survive or flourish without the two operating in tandem and in some kind of syncopated rhythm.

Wonder is at the heart of the matter, as is curiosity and passion.

Too much thinking is coldly analytical and logical in ways that end up missing the soulful aspects of life.

Some academics push a brand of inquiry that is dry, dispassionate and totally logical, as if extracting and ignoring both emotion and intuition will bring us closer to understanding. This is folly.

At the other extreme, we have policy makers who rush forward without gathering facts, evidence and sound intelligence as they pursue a faith-based approach to policy and decision-making.

There must be a way to explore truth and reality without surrendering to either of these extremes.

This book considers the dynamic interplay between dissonance, resonance and insight as questioning and wonder work to resolve the curious aspects of life.

Curiosity did not kill the cat.

That is a silly myth. A dangerous message. A cautionary tale.

Contents

Why question?
Why bother?
Isn't thinking enough?
What's the difference, anyway?
Isn't questioning and thinking part and parcel of the same whole?

No. Not exactly. You can have one without the other.

There is plenty of thinking that never achieves lift-off, never contributes to understanding and never casts light on issues of importance. Much thinking beats around the bush, wanders off course and fails to inform or illuminate.
That is because thinking can be done in an unquestioning manner. Thinking without questioning is like drinking without swallowing. This book promotes the fusion of powerful questioning with thinking.
We must raise young ones to question, to wonder and to learn. We will encourage students to become serial questioners committed to pursuing important questions until capable of making sense of their worlds and fashioning smart answers to life's challenges.

With all the attention paid to thinking and thinking skills by schools, it makes sense to consider how questions and questioning act as decisive elements of the larger operation. Questioning is a possibly potent but often neglected component of the rather amorphous concept referred to as thinking.
Unfortunately, much thinking is done in an unquestioning manner. One can think up a storm, sweat at the forehead and cover lots of ground without learning, without understanding and without making any true headway. One can spin wheels and accomplish little more than a cat chasing her own tail round and round.
Thinking is often proclaimed by state and national leaders as a chief goal of schooling, but the brand of thinking that results from these lofty goal statements may fall short of the mark, amounting to what Shakespeare might call "a tale told by an idiot" or what Pink Floyd might call "another brick in the wall."
Thinking that is guided by intense and strategic questioning is

Why Question?

more likely to lift the thinker above ho hum drum levels that produce little of worth or note. Sadly, much of what poses as thought offers little in the way of wisdom or novelty, creativity or imagination. Much thinking amounts to little more than going through the motions, pondering without generating, and considering without concluding or deciding.

Ironically and paradoxically, a person can spend lots of time thinking without actually qualifying as a thinking person.

At its worst, thinking can resemble a cow chewing its cud.

Many voters, for example, would claim they think before voting even though such thought might be fundamentally lacking in logic, evidence or consideration. One can go through the motions of thought without actually weighing issues or matters of import, without chewing into the facts and data that clarify differences in track records and future prospects for action. Failing to explore the essential questions underlying a major decision like voting leaves the individual more dependent upon conjecture, intuition, gut feelings and whimsey, all of which can sometimes masquerade as thought. Unfortunately, the unquestioning voter is more vulnerable to propaganda and simplistic appeals to fear and prejudice. The demagogue loves the unquestioning voter and the unquestioning citizen because appeals to emotion and fear work well with such audiences.

A student can spend weeks studying an important person from history or literature without actually doing any important thinking, yet it might seem to the casual observer that the student has been thinking long and hard. He or she has turned the pages of many books, highlighted some of the sentences and filled dozens of note cards with key quotations and facts, but in many cases the student is merely collecting factoids with a cut-and-paste strategy that has little to do with significance. This gathering is the consequence of well respected school rituals that elevate hunting and gathering to prominent positions while requiring little questioning.

In contrast, a student should be considering important aspects of the person's life such as these listed at the *Biography Maker* - an online resource I developed to encourage students to focus on matters of import when studying important people. *Biography Maker* is at http://fno.org/bio.html

Biography Questions

1. In what ways was the life remarkable?
2. In what ways was the life despicable?

2

Why Question?

3. In what ways was the life admirable?

4. What human qualities were most influential in shaping the way this person lived and influenced his or her times?

5. Which quality or trait proved most troubling and difficult?

6. Which quality or trait was most beneficial?

7. Did this person make any major mistakes or bad decisions? If so, what were they and how would you have chosen and acted differently if you were in their shoes?

8. What are the two or three most important lessons you or any other young person might learn from the way this person lived?

9. Some people say you can judge the quality of a person's life by the enemies they make. Do you think this is true of your person's life? Explain why or why not.

10. An older person or mentor is often very important in shaping the lives of gifted people by providing guidance and encouragement. To what extent was this true of your person? Explain.

11. Many people act out of a "code" or a set of beliefs which dictate choices. It may be religion or politics or a personal philosophy. To what extent did your person act by a code or act independently of any set of beliefs? Were there times when the code was challenged and impossible to follow?

12. What do you think it means to be a hero? Was your person a "hero?" Why? Why not? How is a hero different from a celebrity?

Unfortunately, thought is easily and frequently held captive by prejudice, preconception, ignorance and closed-mindedness. Some who claim to be thinking are merely turning shopworn ideas and myths over and over again as if turnover had something to do with invention, as if regurgitation had something to do with discovery and insight.

Powerful thought frequently involves boundary breaking, exploration, uncovering, unwrapping and exposure. Breakthrough thinking may engage young ones in questioning authority, challenging conventional wisdom and spawning new beliefs.

We don't need no education.
We don't need no thought control.

"Another Brick in the Wall" by Pink Floyd

Perhaps these uncomfortable aspects of questioning may help to explain some of the wasted time and motion surrounding a thinking

3

Why Question?

curriculum. When rock musicians create songs about bricks in the wall and mind control, we might dismiss them and their satires as hyperbolic reactions of delinquents and dropouts, but embedded in such songs are some disturbing truths about schooling as training for work on assembly lines and fast food restaurants. Pink Floyd's lyrics, along with those of Paul Simon, warn of education as regimentation, transmission of culture and indoctrination. They hint darkly that schooling is too often about compliance, submission and conformity.

> When I think back
> On all the crap I learned in high school
> It's a wonder
> I can think at all
> And though my lack of education
> Hasn't hurt me none
> I can read the writing on the wall
>
> "Kodachrome" by Paul Simon

Pink Floyd warns that even though they "can read the writing on the wall, it doesn't mean anything at all. All in all the words are just bricks in the wall."

Is it possible for a state or nation to promote a thinking curriculum while doing a first rate job of indoctrination all at the same time?

Unfortunately, the answer is affirmative. It is possible to promote thinking without promoting the questioning that infuses the thinking with purpose.

One can learn to think (or color) within the (party) lines.

Mapping Out Zones of Thinking

It may help to clarify the role of questioning as an aspect of thinking to map out the various types and zones of thinking that are included under the broad concept. An appreciation of the dozens of types of thinking and how some end up being little more than cul-de-sacs and diversions will illustrate the central importance of strategic questioning as a way of promoting movement toward understanding.

The first figure on the next page shows several dozen types of thinking that appear ungrouped and uncategorized, but a second version of this figure suggests a grouping pattern. Some types of thinking provoke more originality and actual production than others.

4

Why Question?

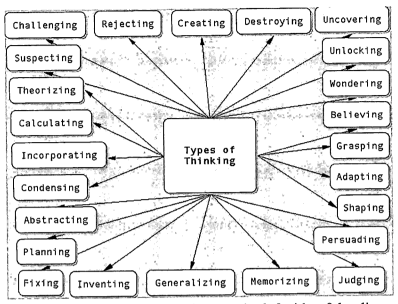

The types of thinking lined up on the left side of the diagram below are the ones that require the least amount of questioning. They all share a focus on memorizing and absorbing rather than generating and producing. If we expect our young ones to become thinkers, capable of developing ideas and insights instead of merely copying

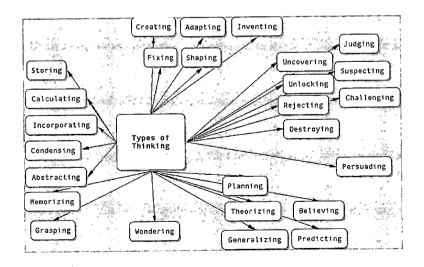

Why Question?

and pasting the thinking or the ideas of others, then questioning becomes paramount, and the importance of the right side of the diagram
becomes evident. Some schools have devoted too much time to the
left side, all the while purporting to teach thinking. This book is
devoted to the proposition that the types of thinking listed on the right
side are critically important in a healthy democracy and a vibrant
society.

The Difference Between Learning and Absorbing

Some confuse absorption with learning, as if students were
sponges soaking up the accumulated wisdom, facts and understandings
of the elders. Many curriculum documents provide lengthy lists of
concepts and information students should absorb - soak up - at various
levels. If one absorbs, does one also understand?

Many definitions of learning and teaching seem focused, sadly, on
this sponge metaphor. It is as if one learns something by digesting it,
by reading it, by hearing it and by committing it to memory.

In many cases, sadly, classroom learning is akin to shelving stock
in a warehouse - just another brick in the wall. It is about accumulating information.

Unfortunately, despite all the talk and the writing about a thinking
curriculum, it may be that some do not expect students to become real
thinkers - those who are capable of fresh thought.

Fresh thought requires that one cope with dissonance, with confusion and with uncertainty. The thinker must fashion new understandings instead of accepting and memorizing the ideas of others. Cutting
and pasting is not sufficient.

The Difference Between Teaching and Learning

It seems as if some schools are too focused on teaching and
instruction instead of learning. These are schools that keep putting
more bricks in the wall. While some might complain that these are
merely matters of semantics, the words carry with them powerful and
controlling implications.

Teaching and instruction tend to focus on the actions of the
teacher transmitting and conveying content to students. A school
committed to student learning on the other hand would focus more
energy on how teachers are orchestrating the questioning, thinking and
discovery of students so they might come up with their own ideas.

In the first school, the teacher might explain the magic of a particular poem and poet to a class, expecting that the students would take careful notes. In the second school, the students might look at the poems and argue over the degree of magic to be found.

While the above sketch is a huge oversimplification of what actually occurs, it does capture a crucial educational divide that usually goes unmentioned.

A few years back I watched three different teachers working with classes in the Louvre.

In the first group a teacher spoke rapidly and energetically about a painting while her 15 year old students wrote down her every word. Even though the painting was hanging right there in front of them, the girls were so busy scribbling they had no time to look at the painting. They had learned, I suppose, that capturing the teacher's words were the secret to scoring well on art appreciation.

In contrast, the neighboring group of 15 year old girls were gazing at a painting spellbound. Neither they nor their teacher did much speaking or writing. The teacher dangled a question and let it hang suspended.

"What questions come to mind as you consider this painting?"

The girls stare intently. Here and there a student scribbles briefly on a note pad then returns to staring.

"Shouldn't we be thinking about his choice of color and his use of light?" asks one girl.

A half dozen girls nod their heads in agreement as the teacher smiles her approval.

"Certainly," she says. "That makes sense to me. What else?"

And a third group across the room listens with full attention as an attractive and charismatic guide speaks enthusiastically in front of a huge battle scene.

This class is made up of senior citizens who do not bother to take notes but hang on each word of their guide as if she is the leading world authority on this artist. With the personal appeal of a movie star she casts a magic light on the painting before them. They have the luxury of feeling rapture while learning, comfortable with the knowledge that there will be no test and the morning will end with a wonderful meal at a bistro accompanied by good red wine.

Questioning as Yeast

Questioning is to thinking as yeast is to bread making. Unleavened bread is flat, hard and unyielding. Unleavened thinking is uninspired.

7

Why Question?

Questioning is what converts the "stuff" of thinking into something of value, acting as leaven to transform matter into meaning.

leaven (NOUN)
An agent that stimulates or precipitates a reaction, development, or change: catalyst, ferment, leavening, yeast. *See* CHANGE. Roget's II: The New Thesaurus, Third Edition. 1995.

The power of this metaphor can be visualized when tracking the relationship between "leaven" and associated terms such as "raise" and "elevate" as shown in the cluster diagram below produced by the Visual Thesaurus at http://www.visualthesaurus.com.

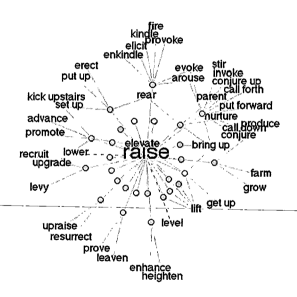

© *2004 Thinkmap, Inc. All rights reserved.*

Note especially, terms such as kindle, elicit, provoke, conjure up, nurture and produce. If only we could raise students capable of such thinking!

At the same time, questioning may act like kneading the dough or

Why Question?

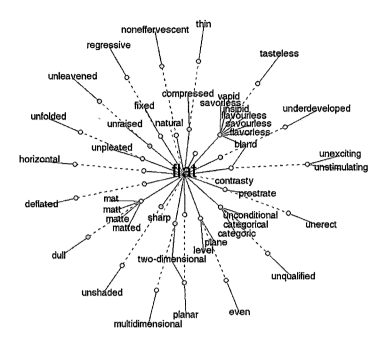

© 2004 Thinkmap, Inc. All rights reserved.

forming it into loaves. The main point here is the importance of lifting thinking beyond the mundane.

The consequences of promoting thinking without due attention to questioning are evident when considering the terms associated with the word "flat" as shown in the diagram on this page produced using the Visual Thesaurus.

Words like insipid, fixed, unqualified, regressive, underdeveloped and dull stand out and serve as a warning that not all thinking proves worthy or worthwhile.

Inattention to questioning condemns the young to collecting, cutting and pasting and servile compliance.

Nurturing a dynamic relationship between questions, wonder and curiosity, on the other hand, frees the young to invent, produce, contribute and adjust to a turbulent and changing world.

Chapter 2 - Why Wonder?

Wondering is about entertaining and exploring possibilities.
It is about hope and faith. It can also be about questioning and doubt . . . Wondering why things are the way they are.

We invite good things to make an appearance. We expect that dreams can make life better. We refuse to settle for less.

"Hold fast to dreams," warned Langston Hughes, "for if dreams die, life is a broken winged bird that cannot fly."

Our sense of wonder - if alive and well - applauds each marvel, each grace, each surprise. We appreciate the extraordinary, the novel and the unique. We hunger for the good, work for the better and hope that the pressures and banalities of life will be supplanted by something more magical. We dream that we can transcend the mundane, that we can escape oblivion, boredom and a life without consequence.

If we are capable of wondering, our mind takes flight and dares to dream. Wondering infuses our questioning and our thinking with a spiritual aspect. Children learn that life can be much more than another brick in the wall

Much of my own thinking about wonder was inspired by reading Rachel Carson's **The Sense of Wonder**, first published by Harper & Row in 1965. As an elementary principal spending lots of time wondering about the dreaming, thinking and questioning of very young children, I found that certain passages resonated intensely with my own impressions and thoughts.

If I had influence with the good fairy who is supposed to preside over the christening of all children, I should ask that her gift to each child in the world be a sense of wonder so indestructible that it would last throughout life as an unfailing antidote against the boredom and disenchantment of later life, the sterile preoccupation with things that are artificial, the alienation from the sources of our strength.

Why Wonder?

The years of early childhood are the time to prepare the soil. Once the emotions have been aroused - a sense of the beautiful, the excitement of the new and the unknown, a feeling of sympathy, pity, admiration or love - then we wish for knowledge about the object of our emotional response.

Once found it has lasting meaning.

It is more important to pave the way for the child to want to know than to put him on a diet of facts he is not ready to assimilate.

If young ones can maintain a sense of wonder as they pass through early childhood into adolescence and early adulthood, that inclination may inspire much of their questioning. As they yearn to understand and make the best of life, a sense of wonder tilts their thinking forward. They grow bolder and stronger in their questioning, testing the edges and boundaries of conventional reasoning, pushing into new territory, demanding fresh truths and answers. They will not see school as a time to memorize time honored answers to multiple choice questions. They will refuse to participate in the "one more brick in the wall" rituals.

But wondering is not a simple joy ride. It has a dark side. The hunger for meaning is not always satisfied. The comfort of memorizing conventional wisdom and platitudes is traded for a much tougher journey, one that often frustrates, teases and disappoints the earnest student. Satisfying, authentic answers are often elusive.

And not all wondering aims high. Students may wonder about trivial matters.

"How long is a tiger's tail?"

"What was the name of emperor's fourth wife?"

Wonder can slip and slide into mere curiosity, just as curiosity can grow into wonderment.

Wondering about fundamental issues and major concerns may take courage and fortitude.

"How can we put an end to war?"

"How can we make sure all children are decently fed and

Why Wonder?

housed?"

"How can we make sure no child is truly left behind?"

These are questions worth wondering about, but answers are unlikely to sprout like spring flowers eager to be picked and displayed. Only the simple minded find simple answers to such profoundly troubling and challenging questions.

Sadly, history is littered with examples of leaders and movements that cut short the wondering and searching for genuine answers to such problems, substituting gimmicks, myths and shadowboxing for real solutions. If the citizens are mentally soft, they may climb right aboard such movements without asking tough questions or wondering whether the proposals make any sense at all.

At its best, wondering combines doubting and dreaming in a powerful partnership to test value. We would hope that all of our young will acquire the inclination and the skills to wonder about the authority of a particular Web site, the reliability of information put forth by a TV or radio station and the worth of a politician's proposal.

Wondering should occur throughout every day of one's life, whether it be about the small issues or the large ones.

"I wonder what's the best way to get around this traffic jam?"

"I wonder what's going to happen in the election today?"

"I wonder how I will adjust if my candidate loses?"

Sadly, wonder can also serve the interests of social control as politicians extending as far back as the Roman Empire have run a circus of one kind or another in order to win the hearts and minds of the populace.

Tribalism, propaganda and marketing depend as much upon magic and wonder as churches, social movements, prophets and revolutionaries. Some of these uses of wonder are heavenly, inspirational and divine, while others are evil to the core, trusting to the power of magic and wonder to sway the feelings and the fears of unsuspecting folk in order to capture their obedience.

A photograph can provoke the most profound emotional reactions, whether they be feelings of wonder or horror. In current times, these images are used repeatedly in the war for human sympathy for one cause or another. The tie between horror and wonder is strong and the distance between them is all too small.

A picture of suffering provokes wondering.

A picture of torture provokes horror.

The younger citizens of this century are bombarded with such images, whether they be about war or deodorant or clothing. One cannot learn about the world without absorbing thousands of images directed at shaping our feelings, wishes, dreams and actions by manipulating our natural sense of wonder.

This book is dedicated to the proposition that wondering without questioning is a form of surrender, a kind of acquiescence in the face of powerful forces far from benign.

The schools of a democratic society are charged with a solemn responsibility to equip the young with questioning skills that support wondering in the best sense, that insulate young ones from propaganda and manipulation.

We should recognize that this goal is not embraced by those powerful figures who profit in various ways from the acquiescence mentioned above. For decades we have seen various groups do what they could to mobilize what political scientists call the mob. Playing upon their fears and baser instincts, these groups on both the left and right have waved flags, provided stirring music and rung bells that were calculated to arouse the hatred, scorn and loyalty of followers.

At its worst this kind of movement leads to gas chambers and death camps. At its extreme edges, this kind of manipulation leads to senseless wars and ethnic cleansing. We see thousands killed and killing in the name of one god or another.

The phenomenon extends across a spectrum from severe to mild.

Social justice can erode as leaders speak disingenuously of compassion, as jobs are sent overseas and international sweatshops sprout up to serve the fashion needs of wealthy nations.

The privileged and affluent young of one nation are swayed by clever advertising to show their personal sense of style by clothing themselves in the latest fashions sewn by those workers in third world nations slaving at $30-$40 per week in conditions that are often unhealthy and dangerous.

Without sharpened questioning skills we and the young may surrender to fashions and movements unknowingly. On the surface, at least, twenty years after **1984** we seem safe from the dangers predicted by the book of that title, but if you scratch that surface and take the time to wonder, to question and to learn, you may doubt that view.

Are we safe?

Has **1984** come and gone?

How can we best teach the young to wonder in ways that will evoke true compassion rather than sham versions?

How can we nurture a sense of wonder that is linked to some universal sense of goodness rather than its evil mirror image?

This book will suggest that questioning is the answer.

14

Chapter 3 - Questions as Technology

Questions and questioning may be the most powerful technologies of all.

North American schools are spending billions bringing networked computers into schools while neglecting the most important technology of all – the ability of students to make meaning by applying sharply honed questioning skills.

This book contends that questions and questioning (mindware) are critically important human technologies that enable young people to solve problems, make smart decisions and score well on the tests of life as well all the other tests that loom in a child's world.

Without strong questioning skills, information technologies contribute little to understanding or insight. There is even some chance that they might dilute understanding and interfere with thinking.

Part One of this chapter explores the importance of questioning while warning against an upsurge of Mentalsoftness™. Part Two proposes a major expansion of school research activities to emphasize daily questioning, exploration and independent thought.

Part One

What is so important about questions and questioning? Questions allow young people to make sense of their worlds and to take action smartly. They are the most powerful tools we have for making decisions and solving problems - for inventing, changing and improving our lives as well as the lives of others.

Questioning is central to learning, growing and acting. An unquestioning mind is condemned to "feeding" on the ideas and solutions of others. An unquestioning mind may have little defense against the *data smog* (Shenk, 1997) so typical of life in this information age. An unquestioning mind is too much like a rudderless sloop swept along by storm swelled currents.

In a democratic society, questions empower citizens to challenge authority to do the most good for the most people.

Questions as Technology

In a fascist society, questions and questioning are viewed with suspicion. Questions are discouraged unless they remain within "safe" zones such as science and technology. We even see concern about questions surface in the first book of the popular Harry Potter children's series as he is denied the right to ask questions by foster parents who find his questioning threatening and disrespectful.

Questions enable the next generations to make changes in society, to invent new and better ways of doing things. They are the mindware that enable us to weigh the value of other tools, determining the best uses for computers, networks, databases, books and other media.

Life is such a puzzle - countless fragments confounding us like a huge jigsaw laid out on the table of our lives.

Each day we return to the table. We struggle to move the pieces around until some picture emerges, until we discover a pattern or a trend, until we can make sense of nonsense. We wrestle with the information flow and flux. We squint. We frown. We dig. We probe. We sift and sort.

We reach into our questioning toolkit to find the right net or scalpel to bring us closer to some truth that may serve us well – provided we have a sufficient toolkit to address the challenge with skill.

The scientific mind does not so much provide the right
answers as ask the right questions.
Claude Lévi-Strauss

Because the new information landscape is streaming by at supersonic speeds, we find ourselves working overtime to "get our minds around" the essential issues, trends and data of our times. Making meaning is harder than ever before.

Supersonic speeds? We open our e-mail and watch a stream of messages flow into our mailboxes. Some of them are correspondence, some of them spam and some of them information "alerts" we have set in motion by subscribing to many of the services that may be tailored to our interests and needs. It is hard to keep up with this torrent.

Quick fixes, wizards and templates abound as substitutes for deeper understanding, but the ultimate answer to information abundance and degradation is unrelenting pondering and questioning. The better we are at interpreting the data and challenging the assumptions behind them, the greater our chances of handling the riddles and the paradoxes that are so prevalent. Questions make it possible.

Questions as Technology

I. Coping with Info-Glut and Charlatans

We live in a world where there is more and more information, and less and less meaning.
Jean Baudrillard
Simulacra and Simulation, 1981

When students turn to their desktops for information, they often find millions of documents within a single "mouse click." Are they worth reading? Will they satisfy their curiosity? Cast light on their biggest concerns?

Looking for financial projections? The future of the stock market? The health of our economy? They uncover thousands. Many were created by amateurs and writers with doubtful credentials. Many predictions contradict the augury of others. Divination is widely practiced but poorly supervised. The Greeks may have done better with their omens, with their seers, prophets and soothsayers, but we must "suffer fools" and wade through the fortune telling and visioning of prophets who are both unlicensed and unschooled.

How can students sort and sift their way past the charlatans and self anointed frauds of this new electronic marketplace? How will they protect themselves from the deceitful?

For those who work in schools, how do we raise young people capable of finding their way through this maze?

Powerful questioning is the answer.

Powerful questioning leads to *Information Power* - the ability to use information to fashion solutions, decisions and plans that are original, cogent, practical and effective.

When students come to a Web page or an online article, they should immediately ask who put it there and whether their ideas can be trusted. They must also challenge the author of a book. What is their background? their experience? their bias? their funding? their track record? their reputation?

None of us can be expert in everything. To some extent we must rely upon others to help us interpret the world, but we must also be wary of "experts" lacking in wisdom, discretion or reliability. We cannot take the time to conduct original, primary source research each time we look for good ideas. We must turn to the sages.

Prior to the Internet, "experts" usually had to pay dues and win various licenses or credentials. It was difficult to win "air time" without passing through some kind of scrutiny or review.

The Internet has made the life of charlatans much easier. We find

17

Questions as Technology

Web sites proudly dispensing hogwash and blather of the worst kind - history that isn't history and medicine that isn't medicine.

We open e-mail "stock tips" from spammers who are paid to recommend securities. We visit search engines and directories that spotlight information that has paid for "shelf space." In the 1950s, this was called "payola" and thought of as bribery. At the start of this new century it is a simple fact of e-commerce that advice is often tainted by conflicts of interests and questionable partnerships.

II. Matters of Definition

Why have we allowed technology companies to misappropriate the word "technology," applying it primarily to tools that plug into the wall and operate on electrical power? Why do we create a special subject area in schools separate from the real classrooms and call it "technology?" Why do we set up skill listings, tests and outcome statements that encourage the use of electronic tools apart from curriculum content?

> *In the animal kingdom, the rule is, eat or be eaten; in the human kingdom, define or be defined.*
> Thomas Szasz

How can anyone justify spreadsheeting divorced from real questions as a worthwhile endeavor? or PowerPointing? or Internetting?

Yet we see this trendy approach to information, to technologies and (almost accidentally) to learning sweeping through schools with little opposition or concern. Being good at technology, we are assured, is crucial if we wish a comfortable future for our children. If they stand a chance at a dot.com job, so the reasoning goes, then they need to be good at technology.

Definitions help to sell product. They carve out territory. They help to establish turf. They focus the spotlight. They shape budgets and priorities. And they sometimes distort planning.

III. Simple Answers to Complex Questions

In all too many cases, the questioning process has been reduced and oversimplified to a search for packaged answers. Artificial intelligence abounds.

Questions as Technology

Questions are intended to provoke thought and inspire reflection, but all too often the process is short circuited by the simple answer or the appealing placebo.

With the advent of new electronic technologies, our young people are threatened by a weakening of thought and an emphasis on the glib or superficial. Mentalsoftness™ is a new social "virus" that is rarely noticed. We hear complaints of a "new plagiarism," but few commentators remark upon the ascendancy of superficial thought.

Around the globe educators report concern that many of the following indicators of Mentalsoftness™ can be observed across the student populations with which they spend their days.

Prime Indicators of MentalSoftness™

1. Fondness for clichés and clichéd thinking - simple statements that are time worn, familiar and likely to carry surface appeal.
2. Reliance upon maxims - truisms, platitudes, banalities and hackneyed sayings - to handle demanding, complex situations requiring thought and careful consideration.
3. Appetite for bromides - the quick fix, the easy answer, the sugar coated pill, the great escape, the short cut, the template, the cheat sheet.
4. Preference for platitudes - near truths, slogans, jingles, catch phrases and buzzwords.
5. Vulnerability to propaganda, demagoguery and mass movements based on appeals to emotions, fears and prejudice.
6. Impatience with thorough and dispassionate analysis.
7. Eagerness to join some crowd or mob or other - wear, do and think what is fashionable, cool, hip, fab, or the opposite or whatever.
8. Hunger for vivid and dramatic packaging.
9. Fascination with the story, the play, the drama, the show, the episode and the epic rather than the idea, the question, the argument, the premise, the logic or the substance. We're not talking good stories or song lines here. We're talking pulp fiction.
10. Enchantment with cults, personalities, celebrities, chat, gossip, hype, speculation, buzz and blather.

Questions as Technology

We know that the most important questions in life defy such formulaic responses. We also know that such recipe books require frequent revision in times of rapid change. Strong questioning skills fuel and steer the inventive process required to "cook up" something new. Without such skills, our students become prisoners of conventional wisdom and the trend or bandwagon of the day.

Synthesis - the development of new possibilities by modifying and rearranging elements - cannot be managed without analysis - the probing, questioning process that explores the underlying principles, characteristics and possibilities of any given situation. Analysis is the underpinning of new thinking and wise choices.

If we hope to see inventive thought infused with critical judgment, questions and questioning must become a priority of schooling and must gain recognition as a supremely important technology. We must lay aside the forked branches of earlier times and the divining rods of soothsayers and futurists. Rather than reading the entrails or taking the omens to determine the future, we wield powerful questions as tools to construct a future of our own choosing.

Part Two – Making Questioning Central to Schooling

Once you have learned how to ask relevant and appropriate questions, you have learned how to learn and no one can keep you from learning whatever you want or need to know.
Neil Postman and Charles Weingartner
Teaching as a Subversive Activity

Smart questions are essential technology for those who venture onto the Information Highway.

Without strong questioning skills, students are mere passengers on someone else's tour bus. They may be on the highway, but someone else is doing the driving.

Without strong questioning skills, students are unlikely to exercise profitable search strategies that enable them to cut past the info-glut, that all too often impedes the search for Insight.

Sometimes this new information landscape seems more like Eliot's **Wasteland** than a library, more like a yard sale than a gold mine. The weaker the questioning and learning skills, the less value one is likely to discover or uncover.

Schools without a strong commitment to student questioning and research are wasting their money if they install expensive networks linking classrooms to rich electronic information resources.

As long as schools are primarily about teaching rather than learning, there is little need for expanded information capabilities. Since many schools and publishers have spent decades compressing and compacting human knowledge into efficient packages and delivery systems like textbooks and lectures, they may not be prepared for a new information landscape that calls for independent thinking, exploration, invention and intuitive navigation.

If districts do not commit as much as twenty-five per cent of their hardware expenditures to curriculum revision and staff development with a focus upon student questioning and research, they are likely to realize little smart use or practice.

1. Prime Questions

Which questions matter most?

Most important thinking requires one of these three Prime Questions:

1. Why?

"Why do things happen the way they do?"

This question requires analysis of cause-and-effect and the relationship between variables. It leads naturally to problem-solving (the How question) or to decision-making (the Which is best? question.)

"Why?" is the favorite question of four-year-olds.

It is the basic tool for figuring stuff out.

At one point while researching student questioning in one prominent district, I found "Why?" occurred most often in kindergarten classrooms and least often in the high school (which had the highest SAT scores in the state.)

"Why does the sun fall each day?"

"Why does the rain fall?"

"Why do some people throw garbage out their car windows?"

"Why do some people steal?"

"Why do some people treat their children badly?"

"Why can't I ask more questions in school?"

2. How?

"How could things be made better?"

This question is the basis for problem-solving and synthesis.

Using questions to pull and change things around until a new, better version emerges.

"How?" is the inventor's favorite question.

"How?" is the tool that fixes the broken furnace and changes the way we get cash from a bank.

"How?" inspires the software folks to keep sending us upgrades and hardware folks to create faster chips.

"How?" is the question that enables the suitor to capture his or her lover's heart.

"How?" is the reformer's passion and the hero's faith.

3. Which?

"Which do I select?"

This question requires thoughtful decision-making - a reasoned choice based upon explicit criteria and evidence.

"Which?" is the most important question of all because it determines who we become.

"Which school or trade will I pick for myself?"

"Which path will I follow?"

TWO roads diverged in a yellow wood,
And sorry I could not travel both
And be one traveler, long I stood

Robert Frost

Faced with a moral dilemma, "Which path will I follow?"

Confronted by a serious illness, "Which treatment will I choose for myself?"

II. What happens in most schools?

There have always been plenty of questions in schools, but most of them have come from the teacher, often at the rate of one question every two to three seconds.

Unfortunately, these rapid fire questions are not the questions we need to encourage because they tend to be recall questions rather than questions requiring higher level thought.

The most important questions of all are those asked by students as they try to make sense out their worlds. These are the questions that enable students to make up their own minds.

Powerful questions - smart questions, if you will - are the founda-

Questions as Technology

tion for AASL's *Information Power*, Barbara Means' *Engaged Learning* and information literacies of all kinds.

Sadly, most studies of classroom exchanges in the past few decades report that student questions are an endangered species.

Information-savvy schools should adopt a basic questioning toolkit and then blend it explicitly into each curriculum area where such skills belong. This toolkit should be printed in large type on posters that reside on classroom walls close by networked, information-rich computers and good books.

Portions of the questioning toolkit should be introduced as early as Kindergarten so that students bring powerful questioning technologies and techniques with them as they arrive in high school.

The Questioning Toolkit

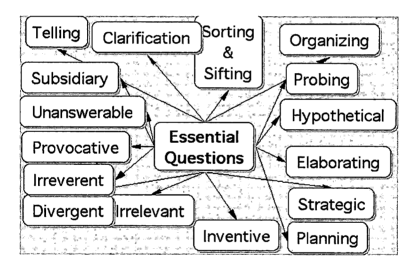

This toolkit is outlined in the next chapter and then a number of succeeding chapters will elaborate on each of the question types.

Questions as Technology

III. Make Questioning a Daily Expectation

Schools should make research and questioning central.

The first step is to make research a daily event in every child's life, not just something that happens once a year in February or March when we suddenly devote several weeks to a state project. Research is the best practice for the kinds of questioning and reasoning described earlier. While there are many ways to increase the frequency of student investigations, the following three strategies are offered as examples of possibilities.

A. The Year Long Project - "Five Hundred Miles"

All students start the year by identifying a leader, a celebrity, a crisis, a hobby or some other aspect of life that interests them enough to devote nine months to its study.

Each student then becomes an expert on her or his subject and is ultimately expected to convert the expertise into an authentic product.

Elements of a Year Long Research Project

1. Selection - Each student settles on one field of interest and identifies one particular aspect worthy of tracking.

2. Questioning - Rather than gathering all information regarding the subject, the student will form key questions so that only pertinent information is retained.

3. Storage - This is an opportunity to design an efficient information storage and retrieval system so that the student can sort, sift and interpret even after collecting hundreds of records.

4. Prospecting - Early in the project, the student surveys the information landscape and identifies all relevant, reliable sites. If possible, the student sets up an automated flow (push technology).

5. Monitoring - The student keeps an eye on daily and weekly developments, periodically visiting sites that have expanding resources but no "alert" capability. The student frequently updates sources as new ones emerge or old ones fold.

6. Responding to inquiries - The student has a chance to demonstrate expertise by responding to questions from peers and others either personally or through e-mail.

7. Creating a product - The student shares insight by developing a product of some kind related to the subject. The product should require original thought, data compression and synthesis. It might be a

report, a presentation, a Web site or some other kind of performance.
A full description of how to manage such projects is online at
http://fno.org/500miles/persistence.html

B. Essential Questions in Every Unit

Each time a teacher introduces a new unit, the class is shown five
or more essential questions and each student is asked to explore one of
them during the unit or build one of her or his own subject to teacher
approval.
These are questions that touch our hearts and souls. They are
central to our lives. They help to define what it means to be human.
Most important thought during our lives will center on such
essential questions.
In the cluster diagram of the *Questioning Toolkit* shown earlier,
essential questions reside at the center of the other types of questions.
Chapter Ten of this book is devoted to this question type.
Essential questions offer the organizing focus for a unit. If the
history class will spend a month on a topic such as Western settlement,
students explore the events and the experience with a mind toward
casting light upon one of the following questions, or they develop
Essential questions of their own . . .

- Why do people move onto other people's lands?
- Are there any decent and good ways to settle on other
  people's lands?
- In what cases did Canadian (or American or Australian)
  settlements violate and damage local peoples?
- How can humans avoid conflicts between cultures that lead to
  pain, suffering, destruction and death?
- Some say Canada (or the U.S. or Australia) still has unfin-
  ished business with regard to settlement. In what ways might
  this claim be true and in what ways untrue? What evidence
  can you supply to substantiate your case?
- If you were Prime Minister (or President), what programs and
  policies would you set in motion to address issues that linger
  with regard to settlement?

C. The Daily Research Question

Teachers greet students each day with an intriguing research
question prominently displayed on the board - puzzles, riddles and

NORTH HIGH SCHOOL
MEDIA CENTER
2222 MICHIGAN AVENUE
WAUKESHA, WI 53188

curious questions that might be answered reasonably well without months of study. These should require some thought and ingenuity and not be trivial pursuits. They should be highly motivating and captivating.

As you proceed through the rest of this book, you will find many more strategies to employ in this effort to make questioning an ongoing, dynamic part of each period of each school day. We are not talking about a token gesture or mere lip service. We are not suggesting a few more bricks in the wall.

The quality of students lives will be enhanced by equipping them with powerful questioning skills so they can learn more than how to read the writing on the wall.

The quality of a society and the well-being of a democracy require that schools counter the cultural drift toward Mentalsoftness™ and lazy thinking with a firm commitment to both questions and questioning.

Chapter 4 - A Questioning Toolkit Revisited

Since the first version of the *Questioning Toolkit* was published in **FNO** in November of 1997 (http://fno.org/nov97/toolkit.html), there has been little revision or elaboration of its major question types and how they might function as an interwoven system of inquiry.

This chapter and this book are intended to take the model quite a few steps further, explaining more about each type of question and how it might support the overall investigative process in concert.

Most complicated issues and challenges require the researcher to apply quite a few different types of questions to the task of building an answer or a solution. These types of questions must be carefully selected to match the task at hand, just as one might pick a saw instead of a hammer when it is time to cut a plank of wood.

The skilled questioner knows which types of questions to ask to accomplish each phase of an investigation and understands how to orchestrate the various types so they work together to bring clarity and understanding to the matter being examined.

Orchestration is the key concept and the primary new element being added to the model with this chapter and this book.

---

orchestrate VERB:
To combine and adapt in order to attain a particular effect: arrange, blend, coordinate, harmonize, integrate, synthesize, unify.
     Roget's II: The New Thesaurus. 1995.

The thinker must consider a number of strategic issues on a continuing basis while gathering information and exploring. On the next page, some of these issues are shown in a cluster diagram. The careful consideration of these issues leads to skillful orchestration rather than haphazard wandering.

As the researcher moves beyond mere gathering to discovering and inventing new meanings, the complexity and the challenge of effective orchestration grows dramatically.

A Questioning Toolkit Revisited

The researcher devotes a great deal of time to questions about the questioning process itself. This questioning about questioning elevates the power of the research process and increases the likelihood that the investigation will lead somewhere fruitful.

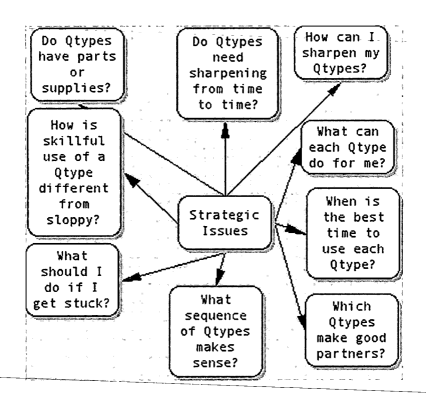

Recognizing the importance and the interplay between these strategies and the various question types (Qtypes) leads to a significant revision of the original *Questioning Toolkit* as can be seen in the diagram on the next page. In the first version, sixteen question types were arranged with the **Essential Qtype** in the center. As orchestration suggests the importance of grouping the question types by function, we see a new pattern emerge with three groups of question types:

1) Qtypes that involve digging (top)
2) Qtypes that involve planning (right)
3) Qtypes that involve invention (bottom left).

A Questioning Toolkit Revisited

This reorganization of the pattern enhances the importance of sequence, function and orchestration.

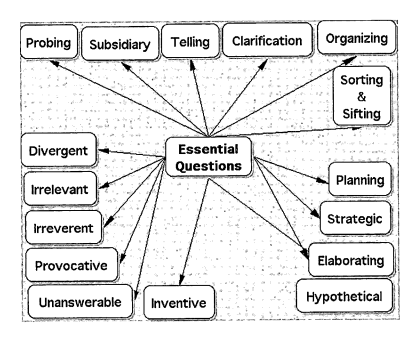

Over the past seven years, I have asked dozens of audiences how they might rearrange the original *Questioning Toolkit*. I am sure that this new version was influenced by the dialogue that took place during those sessions as participants would share their grouping schemes and the reasons for them. To these thinkers I am indebted, and while the grouping pictured above is my own take on this challenge, its birth was certainly inspired by the good thinking of these audiences. I do not offer this grouping as the "correct" version or grouping, as I prefer to think that each thinker will invent a unique and personal toolkit of questioning types that will serve well.

Throughout this book we will explore the significance of each QType alone and in concert, emphasizing strategic questioning aimed at creating new insights as opposed to trivial pursuit or treasure hunts. This is a book about invention and the generation of new knowledge.

We look to schools and teachers to make exploration and inquiry with these kinds of questioning strategies a prime focus of activity so students will emerge from their education as thinkers and inventors, no matter what their choice of vocation and avocation.

A Questioning Toolkit Revisited

If they elect fashion design, we would hope to see them approach the challenge with originality and insight. Not every designer has the chance to invent a swim suit that cuts time off an Olympic swimmer's world record, but there are variations on the theme on every level of the enterprise.

Likewise, if they pick software or hair design, we would hope that they would consider the task with a view toward elegance and harmony. Designing a building? a basket? a flower arrangement? Again, we would hope that they would consider the task with a consideration of simplicity and grace.

I recall a conversation with a carpenter several decades back who helped my family convert a garage into a bedroom for my young daughters. This carpenter spoke of the wood he chose for a staircase railing with a reverence that impressed and surprised me, as his selection came after signing a contract that left little room for top quality lumber. This special wood for the railing would come out of his own pocket. But he approached the room as a creation, almost as a sculptor would. By selecting this wood, he was making his mark as an inventor and an artist. By selecting special wood, he was setting himself apart from that "one more brick in the wall" trap so vividly portrayed by Pink Floyd.

In nearly four decades of working with children in schools, I have come to believe we have expected too little of too many children and have often failed to recognize the potential that nearly all students have to think and perform in magical ways. We have been grading and thinking for too long within the confines of the normal curve, looking for exceptionality at the outer edges rather than assuming its presence along the continuum.

When the normal curve becomes conventional wisdom, schools end up leaving many children behind.

Chapter 5 - Quality Teaching

How do we move past grand theory to effective practice?

What does it take to translate the ambitious goals of this book into daily classroom realities?

Just what is quality teaching? Can the concept cast light on the challenge before us?

A Combination of Elements

These days it is fashionable in many places to focus most of the attention on the science and craft of teaching while neglecting the art and the alchemy. Consideration of the magical aspects of good teaching is all too rare as serious scholars (and politicians) look the other way, showing little interest or faith in such aspects of effective practice. Sadly, a focus on just the scientific aspects of teaching or the so-called research-based aspects leads to an impoverished and inadequate view.

Managing classes with nothing more than the craft and the science of teaching starves students, depriving them of their right to a rich and inspiring educational experience. Such classrooms become wastelands - barren and incapable of nurturing the young.

All four elements shown in the diagram below (craft, science, alchemy and art) are essential.

This call for balance gains acceptance from many classroom teachers who are likely to nod their heads knowingly. While they may prefer the word "magic" to the word "alchemy," teachers know that it

Quality Teaching

takes more than science to spark learning in many students.

Alchemy - Magical aspects of the learning experience that defy science and reason to some extent - the peculiar but often heartening consequences of good chemistry, caring and intuition.

Art - The elevation of practices such as lecturing and questioning to a level full of grace, passion and beauty likely to inspire engagement and deep learning.

Craft - The nitty-gritty, nuts and bolts, how to get the job done techniques of delivering lessons, asking questions, and engaging learners.

Science - Aspects of the learning experience that have been studied to the extent that we can predict with some assurance that if we do X we will get Y as a response or result.

Effective teaching requires a dynamic orchestration of the four aspects listed above, orchestration that cannot be found in any book or score. The teacher must dart and weave, dance and charm.

Hohumdrum teaching leads to stagnation and disappointment.

Spirited teaching provokes, sparks and enlightens.

To nurture the kinds of questioning outlined in this book, we would look for spirited and strategic teaching.

The Challenge: Strategic Teaching

Even though it may be the crux of improving performance, there is little research available touching on the decision-making and judgment required of teachers who seek to apply complex strategies and tactics to novel classroom situations.

The search for science and teacher proof packages cuts against a focus on teachers as inventors and professionals who must juggle complexities.

Each day students walk into a classroom, teachers face novelty. Their training could not completely prepare them for the ever-shifting combinations of personalities, moods and readiness levels that enter the classroom door at 10:10 AM on Tuesday morning. No lesson plan could possibly anticipate the true nature of the day's challenges. Teachers must adapt good intentions and plans rapidly as they diagnose and observe the reactions of their students.

Training models rarely equip teachers to manage these complexities. Techniques may be modeled and practiced extensively, but little is done to prepare teachers for the surprises that are basic to classroom

Quality Teaching

life. Few teachers have ever been given courses in instructional design or strategic teaching.

Stumbling Toward Competence

Little is written about teachers managing skill repertoires, yet it is this juggling and management that can create the best learning opportunities. Part magic, part art, part craft, effective classroom management employs the best of science blended judiciously with intuition and empathy.

Picture teachers acquiring thousands of strategies and tactics during a career. Once they possess a skill, they must hone their command of that skill, applying it to a complicated spectrum of students and situations. Mastery of a specific skill might take years. Training is just the beginning of a long journey.

Each day the teacher considers lesson objectives and strategies before students walk through the door. Once the students appear and the lesson begins, it is usually necessary to shift the lesson plan as the class proceeds and the teacher notes the reactions of various students. In many cases, the teacher must dig deeply into the skill repertoire to find tactics that seem right for the situation that has developed. In some cases, the first new strategies will be successful, but it is a trial-and-error process.

Good teachers effectively "stumble toward competence" as they try out an array of strategies and tactics until they find the right ones. Experience helps to inform their choice of strategies, but novelty stands in the way of any teacher being able to coast along banking on previous experience.

Matchmaking - A Discovery Process

Effective teachers engage in daily matchmaking, creating conditions to promote learning and connecting tasks with students, giving them what they need to be successful while nurturing the process and minimizing obstacles. The best teachers customize lessons so that each student is afforded opportunities that match needs, interests, preferences and skill levels.

If at first you don't succeed . . .

Much of what translates into effective classroom practice must be discovered rather than learned formally in training sessions, yet the discovery process is rarely studied.

We are reminded of the classic story of Robert Bruce watching a spider spinning a web, failing repeatedly but persisting until success-ful. Strong teachers understand that the process of developing effec-tiveness requires great persistence in the face of challenge.

Consistent with the blend of magic, art, craft and science men-tioned above, this chapter offers a dozen strategies for teachers to consider as they plan their personal journeys of discovery and growth. All of these relate to the challenge posed by this book: how can teach-ers best inspire strong questioning, wondering and learning on the part of students.

If we picture the career of a teacher as a lifetime journey, the following strategies will prove instrumental and generative:

1. Increase your magic
2. Understand the young ones
3. Look for good routines
4. Avoid heroics
5. Take breaks - coast - rest - pace yourself
6. Ask for help, for ideas, for tricks
7. Question
8. Add one strategy each week
9. Focus
10. Project like a champion - Have faith
11. Lose weight - shed the nonsense
12. Eat well - feed yourself on good ideas

1. Increase your magic

The success of a teacher depends to some extent upon magic and alchemy - the ability to do some or all of the following:

• Spark learning
• Cast spells
• Awaken thirst
• Captivate
• Charm
• Delight
• Disarm
• Deliver (In the sense of setting free.)

Unfortunately, there is little in the formal preparation of teachers that would equip them to succeed with this aspect of quality teaching. It is rare to find a teacher who was offered a course in presenting a captivating lecture or a course in capturing the hearts and minds of students. This dimension is often ignored and neglected by formal pre-service programs, but it is often a deciding factor in how students respond to classroom challenges and teachers.

How does a teacher increase magic?

In most respects, the task resists training and methodology.

Imagine courses offering to teach virtual sincerity.

Charm school for teachers?

Actually, the learning process probably starts on a very individual and personal level as a teacher acknowledges that human chemistry and magic are prime elements in learning. Once the teacher embraces that notion, the search begins. Is charisma and chemistry an accident of birth? Can they be developed?

To some extent, magic in the classroom is a matter of mastering tricks of the teaching trade, much like card tricks and sleight of hand. But those tricks and tactics are a subset of a larger and probably more important range of magical effects, those concerned with the human chemistry and relationships of the classroom. These should not be a result of trickery and sleight of hand.

In many cases, the warmth we see in a particular classroom was probably kindled over several months as the teacher greeted the students each day, showed interest in their lives outside the classroom, discovered their personal concerns and passions and demonstrated an appreciation and empathy that seemed genuine. Chances are this foundation was then amplified on a class by class basis by the teacher building a bridge for the students between their concerns and the content at hand, bringing the history or the math to life in vivid terms.

We can learn some of this by watching and reading, but much of the learning requires experimentation. Deep magical connections are rooted in primal human communications such as eye contact and emotional vulnerability.

If someone is bad at eye contact, how do they get better?

When the adult teacher is a closed and guarded person, magic is a stretch. The more authoritarian the teacher, the less likely magic will occur. The challenge of increasing magic may be outside the reach of policy as it depends fundamentally upon human dynamics and choices that are more individual than institutional.

We can increase magic in schools by hiring more magical teachers and by providing support for individual teachers to work on this aspect of their profession, but we cannot easily legislate these changes.

Policy makers might address the conditions of a teacher's life that interfere with the creation of magic as heavy class loads and piles of

Quality Teaching

bureaucratic tasks can tax the energy of teachers in ways that put them in a survival mode from which little magic is likely to emerge. At the same time policies such as high stakes testing and punishment are likely to dilute magic as schools start to act more and more like fast food restaurants treating students like hamburger patties.

Each teacher makes a personal choice. When making magic a priority, a teacher opts for a career that may bring amazing psychic rewards. These teachers find that teaching is about releasing human potential and working transformations. By tapping into the spiritual dimension of learning, these teachers open themselves to the greatest possible rewards, but there is a dark side to such openness, since not all efforts succeed and not all students respect the vulnerability.

2. Understand the young ones

Effective teachers work very hard to understand who the students really are, to uncover their hopes, fears, wishes, dreams and trials in order to get to the heart of the matter. By personalizing the classroom and the search for meaning, they win loyalty and effort.

Intimate knowledge of individual students is a basic element of good practice, but it is not enough to wish that every teacher develop such knowledge. There are resource and policy issues that stand in the way of intimacy, as certain instructional modes are mechanized, standardized and heavily scripted. It is all too fashionable in some quarters to apply a "one size fits all" approach to pedagogy, a fashion that works against establishing the very intimacy and customization of learning opportunities most likely to transform the performance of under-performing students.

3. Look for good routines

Critics often make it seem that schools are plagued by dull routines and dull teachers, but good routines are an essential aspect of surviving the pressures and chaos that often characterize life in schools. We should honor the value of good routines and support those teachers who commit to refreshing their routines.

Effective teachers acquire thousands of tricks of the trade - classroom moves and tactics - strategies to induce learning and achieve good results. This vast repertoire of strategies provides a rich and varied choice of interventions so that the teacher can make the good matches mentioned earlier between learners and learning opportunities.

Quality Teaching

The process of adding to the repertoire should go on throughout one's entire career, as a good teacher keeps looking for ways to enhance effectiveness and continues to seek information about new challenges such as the arrival of a new group of immigrants.

It is not enough to read about a new routine or see it demonstrated in a workshop. The teacher must adapt it, practice it, adapt it some more and manage to fit it into the life of the classroom in a way that is comfortable and consistent with other routines. The process is akin to honing or whetting a knife blade until perfectly sharp.

4. Avoid heroics

Heroics sometimes lead to excesses and a kind of dominance likely to undermine the very independence we seek to encourage on the part of our students. If we do too much for them or become the winds in their sails, we do them no favors.

At times the strategies advanced in this article may appear to conflict with each other, but that is because teaching requires an appreciation of paradox as well as a tolerance for ambiguity. Thus we see that heroics can get a teacher in trouble, yet later we argue that effective teachers project like champions. How does an individual reconcile these two seemingly contrary recommendations? The answer of course, is a matter of judgment, of balance and emphasis.

When the teacher goes out on a limb and becomes overextended, the energy required to reach students and achieve results becomes depleted and the level of stress is so high that it easy for the teacher to slip into patterns of behavior that are actually counterproductive.

Modulation is key to success.

We look for balance . . . inspiration that leads to self sufficiency.

Students learn to light their own fires, pose their own questions and pursue truth with a fervor and determination that is resolute.

5. Take breaks

Teaching is a bit like running a marathon. Pacing is essential. In order to restore the reserves necessary to fuel passionate teaching, teachers must learn to coast and take advantage of plateaus.

Sadly, coasting has been given a bad name and is seen as slacking by many outside the profession. If only we ran our schools like buzzing factory floors with rewards for frenzied activity, the argument goes . . .

Quality Teaching

As with many of the helping professions, burnout is a risk for teachers who run too fast and forget to take care of their own needs. Managing the energy flow in and out of the psychic system is basic to survival, yet little is done to prepare young teachers for this aspect of career management.

Current educational policies that seek school improvement by increasing threat and stress are wrong-minded.

Chances are the high pressure school reform approaches of this decade will be seen by history as a kind of educational version of what has been called the "Dark Ages" as those outside the profession have sought to improve performance by meddling with a profession that they little understand.

6. Ask for help

How strange that some reformers push schools to become more competitive. Growth and change are more likely to thrive in more collaborative cultures. When teachers gather in mutually supportive communities of practice, trading good techniques, exchanging stories of change and experimenting together, they stand a good chance of advancing their skill levels and persisting through difficult trials. In contrast, the isolation that too often characterizes school cultures undermines performance and growth.

In some schools, asking for help is seen as weakness.

In some schools, sharing successful strategies is seen as endangering merit pay rewarded for outstanding scores.

Quality teaching is demanding and exhausting, often frustrating and painful. Fellowship can play a major role in validating one's worth as a teacher during the toughest moments but it can do more than that. Just as partners and ropes permit rock climbers to scale seemingly impossible peaks, team support can give teachers the lift they need to reach optimal levels of performance.

7. Question

When we stop questioning, we stop learning and growing.

At the end of a day of teaching, many teachers reflect on the hours that have passed, rewinding the tape to consider what worked, what did not. This reflective process is central to the growth process, and questions are the tools that enable the following to thrive:

• Wondering

- Considering
- Predicting
- Challenging
- Testing
- Probing
- Stretching
- Inventing

Ideally, the questioning teacher becomes capable of reinvention and is never stuck for long in ruts.

Because this book is devoted to powerful questioning, it should prove valuable to teachers who wish to enhance their capacities in this respect.

When teachers stop questioning their own practice, they lose touch with their students and the learning process.

Questioning leads to adaptation and personalization.

At a time when standardization is the fashion, questioning runs against the grain.

"Do as we say."

"Follow orders."

"Follow the script."

8. Add one strategy each week

From theory into practice . . .

It takes time to understand, to test, to adjust and to adapt each new strategy until it fits comfortably into daily practice. If a teacher sets the goal of adding one new strategy a week, it may prove too ambitious, for the process of skill acquisition may extend over several weeks for each new strategy, but the conscious personal commitment to building one's repertoire is central to the model of quality teaching advanced by this chapter.

Quality teaching amounts to a lifetime journey of exploration, practice and discovery.

9. Focus

Quality is enhanced by digging down deeply into particular aspects of performance rather than spreading oneself thin and emerging as dabbler and piddler. A teacher might identify one major category to enhance such as questioning, for example, and could easily spend an entire year just modifying lessons using strategies such as the *Question Press*. (**FNO** article, February-March 2004 at http://fno.org/feb04/questionpress.html)

This book would serve as a handbook to support such a year of focus on effective pedagogy along with other books that will be suggested later.

In a similar vein, a teacher with a load of 150 students each day might select a half dozen especially worthy students for special effort during a period of days and weeks. There may be several students going through special difficulties. Others might need a nudge. Some may be on the verge of a break through. The teacher invests heavily and strategically in a half dozen or more students to set in motion good works of various kinds.

If we concentrate on deep and major effects, teachers are more likely to make a difference.

10. Project like a champion

In contrast with the earlier section warning against heroics, this section urges the teacher to communicate faith, encouraging young ones by example and modeling. The job of the teacher is, to some extent, to defy the odds and unleash human potential that might have been, for one reason or another, been blocked.

• Have faith
• Encourage
• Model
• Inspire
• Challenge
• Reach
• Extend
• Defy

The teacher is primarily responsible for equipping young ones with the tools, the spirit and the knowledge to take flight and handle life with independence and skill.

One of the most important aspects of this challenge has to do with attitude and spirit.

Teachers can make a huge difference in a child's sense of self, encouraging or discouraging, equipping or neglecting. We would hope to defy society's expectations and transform the weak student from disadvantaged origins into a capable, self-assured producer.

Quality Teaching

"You write very well," she said.
"Your drawings are full of such color and feeling . . . :
"You showed such good effort here."
"I think you have a great future."

11. Lose weight - shed the nonsense

As the teacher adopts new routines and expands the teaching repertoire, the acquisition of new techniques should be accompanied by a shedding and pruning process as the teacher identifies the practices and programs that have failed.

The goal is to eliminate all but the worthy.

Questioning is at the heart of this process, as the teacher asks what is worth keeping and what needs to be pruned.

12. Eat well

Another paradox! How can we talk about eating well and losing weight in the same breath?

It is all about avoiding empty calories and feasting on ideas that are lean and nurturing at the same time.

- Feed yourself on good ideas.
- Establish and maintain a robust flow of promising techniques.
- Go far afield in search of novelty.
- Balance novelty with bread and butter basics

How do we move past grand theory to effective practice?

This chapter suggests an approach that is at odds with much of the top down public policy currently fashionable. We will see the best results when we are able to create a solid balance between the four elements mentioned in the beginning. We need to work on the art and magic of teaching as well as the science and the craft of teaching. Policy makers must also devote themselves to the broader social issues and working conditions that contribute to school failure.

Chapter 6 - Learning Questioning 1

Questioning combines a set of strategies with related attitudes that may be acquired and developed over many years. The acquisition process can go on for decades, extending from early childhood into later years as some keep sharpening their questioning faculties right up until the very end of the lives while others seem to glide along without much effort in that regard.

Questioning is an inclination as well as an action - a predisposition to challenge, explore and discover. Throughout this book we applaud the serial questioner - one who explores an important issue with a dogged determination. The original essential question gives birth to dozens of related questions that in turn spawn hundreds more.

Fueled by this spirit of inquiry, the serial questioner applies a rich repertoire of strategies to the quest for understanding. Moving through life from sandbox to workplace and community, first as child, later as adult, the serial questioner will keep acquiring thinking and inquiry skills. Thirst for more is never satisfied or quenched.

Much of this questioning may first be learned at home as parents cultivate both spirit and skills before kindergarten, but schools and good teachers will extend and deepen what families may have started. If families have not, for one reason or another, nurtured the questioning at home, then schools must work extra hard to close the gap. Finally, the most important learning of questioning will be the responsibility of the learner. The most profound growth will be self-generated as the questioner becomes devoted to acquisition, adding layer upon layer of skill sets in a complex web.

I. The Demands of Complex Questions

Most important questions require the skillful pursuit of a series of subsidiary questions, yet in school students are often trained to consider Q/A pairs.

Question ——> Answer
Question ——> Answer
Question ——> Answer
Question ——> Answer

Learning Questioning 1

Life is rarely so simple or so cooperative.

When we explore what Michael Leunig calls "the difficult truth," we must learn to live with entire families of questions - whole generations of them spawned by a central or essential question. At times, this spawning appears to spiral out of control as dozens and dozens of questions emerge.

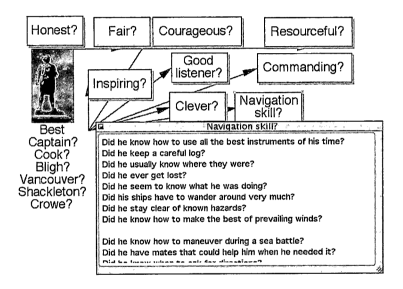

One question leads to another and another and another.

The search for understanding and insight is exhausting, especially since we cannot find or uncover answers to the main questions. We must gather answers to the smaller (subsidiary) questions and then construct answers to the more important questions by synthesizing what we have gathered.

We learn to combine a dozen stories of treachery and deceit to build a case for a captain having a flaw.

- Was he fair to the people he encountered on his journeys?
- What do you mean by "fair?"
- What did "fair" mean then?
- Are there stories of encounters that might help us decide?
- Can we trust the versions that have survived this much time?

Learning Questioning 1

The pursuit of these complex webs of questions requires a commitment to what may prove to be a long and often frustrating search. It is this predisposition that sets the serial questioner apart from the mentally lazy who are content with second hand truths.

Attitudes and Traits of the Serial Questioner

Most of us grew up with the simple Q/A approach, as teachers tended to dominate classroom exchanges with brief Q/A exercises with wait time of less than 3 seconds.

Classroom discourse was often about recall rather than exploration, and school research, all too often, was about gathering rather than building answers or fashioning solutions.

Serial questioning is something quite different.

A serial questioner possesses a number of remarkable traits and propensities that may be nurtured by parents, teachers, schools and mentors of various kinds.

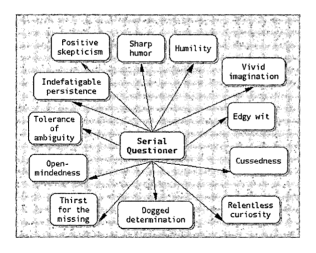

1. Humility

Arrogance blocks understanding.

If you think you know all the answers, chances are good that the most important ones will elude you. The serial questioner is ready and willing to acknowledge a lack of certainty and an appetite to learn more. Question begets question much like a virulent strain of virus.

Learning Questioning 1

Ironically, those who feast on *umble pie* are more likely to get to the heart of the matter. The origin of umble pie:

The pie referred to in 'eating humble pie' was really umble pie, made from the umbles - heart, liver and gizzard - of a deer. It was made to be eaten by servants and huntsmen, while the lord of the manor and his guests dined on venison.
Source: Morris Dictionary of Word and Phrase Origins
(second edition, Harper Collins, Publishers)

2. Relentless Curiosity

Curiosity, despite the old saying to the contrary, did not kill the cat. Where did that saying come from, anyway? Why do we share such a disturbing message with children? Do we really want them to grow up compliant and disengaged?

Parents and schools must encourage curiosity, awaken it when sleeping and reward it when emergent. Curiosity fuels invention and discovery. Without curiosity we have detachment and boredom.

The serial questioner is always wondering why and how and whether.

3. Indefatigable Persistence

The pursuit of understanding rarely pays off handsomely, rapidly and easily. These inquiries are not entertainments like pulling the arm of a slot machine or dropping coins into arcade games. Wrestling truth from the jungle of information available with all the twists and turns, biases and distortions typical of many sources, can be very frustrating, often tedious and usually prolonged. This is not about Play Stations™ and TinkerToys™.

Because insight is elusive and the search may be difficult, persistence - the ability to stay the course - is paramount. It is a matter of spirit and character. Unlike Trivial Pursuit® and various treasure hunt games, inquiry into difficult questions is like slogging through mud or briar patches. The student must be steadfast. Roget's equates "indefatigable" with "Having or showing a capacity for protracted effort, regardless of difficulty or frustration: inexhaustible, tireless, unfailing, unflagging, untiring, unwearied."

4. Dogged Determination

The serial questioner burns the late night candle down to the nub. As all the other lights turn off and the seeking stops, the serial questioner cannot sleep and cannot rest. The unanswered question is a powerful mistress, capable of inspiring an almost obsessive commitment. The researching student is stubbornly persevering and tenacious.

5. Open-mindedness

As much as possible, the serial questioner sheds preconceptions prior to research, taking off filters that might block discoveries.

(The next portion on open minds is adapted from **Administrators at Risk: Tools and Technologies for Securing Your Future**, McKenzie, 1993.)

What is an open mind? A mind that welcomes new ideas. A mind that invites new ideas in for a visit. A mind that introduces new ideas to the company that has already arrived. A mind that is most comfortable in mixed company. A mind that prizes silence and reflection. A mind that recognizes that later is often better than sooner. An open mind is somewhat like Silly Putty®. Do you remember that wonderful ball of clay-like substance that you could bounce, roll and apply to comics as a child?

An open mind is playful and willing to be silly because the best ideas often hide deep within our minds away from our watchful, judgmental selves. Although our personalities contain the conflicting voices of both a clown and a critic, the critic usually prevails in our culture. The critic's voice keeps warning us not to appear foolish in front of our peers, not to offer up any outrageous ideas, and yet that is precisely how we end up with the most inventive and imaginative solutions to problems. We need to learn how to lock up the critic at times so the clown can play without restraint. We must prevent our internal critic from blocking our own thinking or attacking the ideas of others.

An open mind can bounce around in what might often seem like a haphazard fashion. When building something new, we must be willing to entertain unusual combinations and connections. The human mind, at its best, is especially powerful in jumping intuitively to discover unusual relationships and possibilities. An open mind quickly picks up the good ideas of other people, much like Silly Putty® copying the image from a page of colored comics.

47

Learning Questioning 1

The open mind is always hungry, looking for some new thoughts to add to its collection. The open mind knows that its own thinking is almost always incomplete. An open mind takes pride in learning from others. It would rather listen than speak. It loves to ask questions like, "How did you come up with that idea? Can you tell me more about your thinking? How did you know that? What are your premises? What evidence did you find?"

The open mind has "in-sight" - evaluating the quality of its own thinking to see gaps that might be filled. The open mind trains the clown and the critic to cooperate so that judgment and critique alternate with playful idea generation. Ideas have at least three major aspects that can usually be modified and improved:

1. Ideas are based upon premises of one kind or another. Many people come to their ideas without ever explicitly examining the premises that lie underneath those conclusions. Premises are basic beliefs that act for an idea as the foundation of a building or the roots of a tree. Collections of premises are often called assumptions or mind-sets. Sometimes our thinking comes to us already packaged without our even knowing which premises and assumptions lie below the surface, but an open mind knows that all such premises must be reexamined with some frequency to see if they are serving us well and truly match our basic belief systems.

2. Ideas are based upon evidence. Many of our ideas emerge from experience. We collect data, look for patterns and seek laws to help us predict the future. Unfortunately, we all too often collect evidence selectively. Once people begin to hold an idea, research has shown that they begin to screen out data which might create dissonance, evidence which might call into question the value of the idea. An open mind looks at the quality of its evidence with the same dispassionate attitude it applies to its premises and assumptions. Mindful of the three little pigs who built houses of straw, twigs and brick, the open mind seeks bricks and mortar that can withstand the huffing and puffing of the most aggressive wolf.

The open mind asks, "What evidence do I need to gather? Do I know enough? Has anything changed since I last gathered evidence? Is there new data? Is my data complete?"

3. Ideas may also be based upon logic. Our conclusions and ideas should flow from logical connections between our premises and our evidence. The open mind keeps asking of its ideas, "Is this logical? Does this make sense? Does this follow from the evidence I gathered? Have I identified all the key factors?

6. Tolerance of Ambiguity

Ironically, while we seek clarity and understanding, complex questions usually defy our wishes and the search for meaning may feel like sailing through thick fog banks with only occasional glimpses of light and shoreline.

Raised on a diet of canned research projects and science experiments, many students will initially expect smooth sailing in broad daylight, and they may soon tire of the fog, complaining that the research is "dumb" or "stupid."

Many cultures now promote simplistic, "black and white" thinking - suggesting that difficult issues can be solved by applying slogans and various sugarcoated pills. The struggle for political power has collapsed into a contest of sound bites and mind candy as candidates propose solutions to quandaries that fit neatly into 30 second TV ads. Because sacrifice and patience are thought to be in short supply, citizens are spoon fed platitudes and bromides.

The best solutions to complicated situations often require an appreciation of nuance and subtlety. Learning to recognize the gray of life - the ambiguity - and to adjust plans accordingly is part of living in the real world as opposed to the false world of ideologues and demagogues who sell simple solutions and false hope. Certainty is often a warning sign of ignorance masquerading as something finer.

7. Thirst for the Missing

What we do not know is often just what we need to know. What we do not understand is usually at the heart of the matter. Truth often lurks in the shadows - the negative space and the darkness of life. When we restrict our search to the well lit spaces, we risk blinding by the light.

The serial questioner wonders what she or he may have overlooked. The apparently irrelevant question often proves crucial. There are many twists in the road capable of throwing even the best detective off track.

8. Positive Skepticism

The healthy skeptic is inclined to find out what is substantial and what is credible. Doubt works like a sculptor's chisel, carving away at the surface and scraping away facades and veneers until the researcher finds something plausible. Positive skepticism intends to resolve doubt and put aside reservations. The researcher moves toward conviction.

9. Sharpened Humor

Humor:
The ability to perceive, enjoy, or express what is amusing, comical, incongruous, or absurd.
The American Heritage® Dictionary of the English Language: Fourth Edition. 2000.

Someone unable to notice the humor in things is unlikely to look for or find the truth.

"There is something funny going on here."
Funny:
1a. Causing laughter or amusement. b. Intended or designed to amuse. 2. Strangely or suspiciously odd; curious. 3. Tricky or deceitful.
The American Heritage® Dictionary of the English Language: Fourth Edition. 2000.

We are inclined to think about the comical side of humor without paying homage to the aspects that inspire exploration and discovery. Noticing the incongruous awakens our curiosity and sets in motion the search for resolution. Suspecting the deceitful inspires the investigation.

10. Edgy Wit

The serial questioner has a mind capable of cutting through all manner of underbrush, confusion, propaganda, marketing, smog and fog. Questions are the tools for probing and exploring. Sharp edged at times and blunt at other times, questions enable us to exercise our wit.

Wit:
1. The natural ability to perceive and understand; intelligence. 2a. Keenness and quickness of perception or discernment; ingenuity. Often used in the plural: living by one's wits. b. wits Sound mental faculties; sanity: scared out of my wits. 3a. The ability to perceive and express in

an ingeniously humorous manner the relationship between
seemingly incongruous or disparate things. b. One noted
for this ability, especially one skilled in repartee. c. A
person of exceptional intelligence
The American Heritage® Dictionary of the
   English Language: Fourth Edition. 2000.

Delving into complex issues requires an array of digging strategies such as the following:

Beat the bushes, bore, burrow, cultivate, culture, cut, dig,
dig out, dike, dredge, dress, drill, drive, excavate, explore,
fertilize, forage, force, frisk, furrow, go through, gouge,
gouge out, groove, grub, harrow, hoe, hollow, hunt, list,
look around, look round, look through, lower, mine,
mulch, nose around, plow, pocket, poke, poke around,
prune, pry, quarry, rake, research, root, sap, scoop, scoop
Source: The Thesaurus at HyperDictionary.Com

11. Vivid Imagination

"Picture that!"

If you could not imagine the Grail, it would be difficult to seek it.
Moving civilization and culture forward involves the picturing of
new lands, new possibilities and new ideas. Often we cradle these
infants in our "Mind's Eye," wary of premature birth. We toy with
potentials and possibilities on the off chance that one or more might
survive the winnowing process and prove valuable.

12. Cussedness

WordNet Dictionary
Definition:
[n] mean-spirited disagreeable contrariness
Synonyms: orneriness
See Also: contrariness, perverseness, perversity
Disputatiousness and perversity (what the Americans
call "cussedness"). —James Bryce.
Webster's 1913 Dictionary

Those who challenge conventional wisdom and the prized beliefs of the day are usually painted as heretics, nonconformists and malcontents. Their criticism and contentiousness are rarely welcomed. They, like whistle-blowers, are often shunned, exiled and pilloried.

This being the case, it takes an unusual spirit to stand up and point to naked emperors or false prophets. It requires courage to accuse a Joe McCarthy of demagoguery as did Edward R. Murrow during the 1950s:

We will not walk in fear, one of another. We are not descended from fearful men, not from men who feared to write, to speak, to associate and to defend causes which were for the moment unpopular. This is no time . . . to keep silent.

We must not confuse dissent with disloyalty.

The serial questioner is not easily turned aside and away, is not readily satisfied with half truths and blandishments. Platitudes and bromides simply inspire renewed questioning.

Giving Birth to Serial Questioners

The attitudes and behaviors outlined in this chapter and the next are most likely to thrive when they are a clear goal of the home and the school working in partnership.

When questioning is prized by the adults, the young are encouraged to pursue their passions and curiosities. They are given frequent opportunities to explore, discover and invent.

While rules, expectations and boundary lines are important in such families and schools, the young are also encouraged from time to time to color outside the lines and explore outside the boundaries of conventional thought. They are taught to exercise judgment when testing limits and exploring outside the norm.

In some families and some schools, such exploration is forbidden and discouraged. The young are not allowed to exercise discretion. The walls are thick and high. It is about these schools that Pink Floyd was singing with "Another brick in the wall."

This chapter emphasized attitudes. The next will focus on skills.

Chapter 7 - Learning Questioning 2

What skills should accompany the attitudes outlined in the previous chapter?

A hunger for answers amounts to little if we cannot equip the young with the tools to dig, delve and divine the truth. This is not a matter of divining rods or magic wands - rather an array of questioning and thinking strategies that make exploration, discovery and invention possible.

This chapter reviews more than a dozen strategies that are crucial but all too often neglected by schooling and programs that profess to teach thinking.

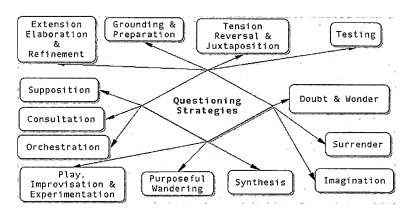

1. Orchestration

Chief among the strategies in the diagram above would be the smart selection and orchestration of question types - an understanding of when each question type should be applied to the challenge at hand.

Thinkers cannot rely upon recipes, scripts or prescribed patterns. They must often make up their approach as they proceed. Each important quest or investigation requires customization and adaptation. The thought process, if it could be captured visually, might appear like a pinball bouncing from point to point, as the mind darts and weaves from here to there, trying first one and then another tack. Or the thought process might resemble a flock of sloops cutting back and forth across the wind. Or sometimes it might look more like a fireworks display, a shooting star, a cat chasing its tail or a dust devil spinning and spinning intently across apparently barren earth.

Just as those who conduct orchestras will bring each section into the performance at the right time and right tempo - horns, woodwinds, strings and percussion all in their places - the thinker must do some of the same directing, playing with dissonance, resonance, harmony and other aspects of idea flow, contrast and conflict to generate the sparks, energy and illumination required to fashion new meanings. In contrast with the conductor, however, the thinker's work is fundamentally improvisational with hardly any score or sheet music to guide the exploration. The process is often intuitive and whimsical rather than strictly linear, logical or sequential with the mind dancing about in ways that sometimes seem errant, absurd and distracted.

The thinker must nurture the magical aspects of exploration while tempering those tendencies with occasional doses of logic and analysis. Above all, then, the thinker must be conscious of some of the process, at least part of the time, occupying a mental crow's nest to view the action on the brain's "deck," intervening from time to time to stimulate, redirect or manage the discovery process.

Over the years, schools have rarely invested in showing young ones how to manage this kind of thinking, with the possible exception of some efforts that emerged along with the gifted education movement during the 1980s, but many of those efforts leaned rather heavily on the logical, analytical and structured processes without enough attention to the more intuitive aspects of creative production.

We might turn to jazz musicians for one source of inspiration as we consider the meaning of the statement, "Now you're cookin." While a jazz performance may follow a basic melody line to some extent, the musicians often play all around those lines and wander far afield, allowing their instincts and feelings to weave magical sounds that emerge on the spur of the moment.

Keith Jarrett, a jazz pianist who was long known for exceptional improvisation, once described how much each audience could shape an evening's performance as he would enter the concert hall, feel the energy of the group and find music actually passing through him and his fingers into the piano and then back into the room.

Writers and visual artists often speak or write of inspiration in similar terms, as if they are the vehicle for something outside that flows through them. The Greeks and Romans tried to capture some of this phenomenon with figures like the Muses, and creative thinkers, artists and performers have been seeking their Muses for centuries since that time. Sadly, some seek them in the bottom of bottles, in clouds of smoke or in heated spoons.

The powerful recent movie, "Ray," paints a compelling portrait of Ray Charles struggling with musical invention, fame and drug addiction as he rose to the tops of the charts and changed the landscape of American music. Ray Charles was a talented imitator, but the film shows his career limping along until he moved towards more originality.

It requires an odd combination of surrender and management to harness these tremors, glimmers and possibilities in ways that show up in writing, art or performance without losing one's grip and succumbing to the temptations and diversions that haunted Ray Charles and threatened to derail his life and work.

How can this best be learned?

It helps to share healthy stories of invention, imagination and creativity while children are still very young, identifying the positive elements as they evolved during the lives of good writers, musicians, artists and others.

Once familiar with the stories, children can be engaged in creative tasks that require a balance between surrender and control, using watercolor washes, for example, to paint a sunset.

Watercolor has a way of flowing somewhat independently from the artist's intent so that good painters learn to play with that errant quality and use it to good advantage. Others try to dominate the medium in ways that constrain its power and possibilities, superimposing techniques that might work better with oil and canvass.

Trite as the expression has become, "Go with the flow!" captures some of the spirit, mood and stance we hope to engender. Unfortunately, many activities launched in schools may rely a bit upon templates, models and patterns that do little to provoke the kind of playful spirit actually required to produce something original and noteworthy.

Roger von Oech has written some of the best books about this process. His **Whack on the Side of the Head** identifies the many mental locks that can block creative production.

2. Supposition

Why do you suppose?
How do you suppose?

55

Learning Questioning 2

What might happen if?
To a large extent, inventive thinking involves informed guess work, hypothesis testing and speculation. The thinker attempts to construct a theory and then tests to see if it matches reality. This process works best if one is conscious of the construction and testing while it proceeds. One plays with possibilities, tugging first this way and then that way until some semblance of order and sensibility emerges.

Much of this work begins with cognitive dissonance, the recognition that some aspect of life or society is tilted awry or in need of attention. We wonder how we might set things straight, make them better, address a grievance or right a wrong. We ask what might happen if . . .

The search for a new way, an improved approach or a solution to a problem is in some respects an attempt to brings things into harmony, to establish a degree of resonance. We try to transform what is chaotic, confused or disordered into something more regular, more patterned and more sensible.

Supposition is closely associated with imagination - the ability to picture things differently.

3. Imagination

Imagine that!

The thinker must be able to conceive of new possibilities, variations, combinations and twists to reshape reality and move the culture forward. Even though some claim that "there are no new ideas under the sun," novelty is a persistent and formative aspect of modern society, one that is often prized in the work place and the community. Countering the pessimism of "no new ideas" would be sayings about variety as the spice of life and the importance of originality.

The principal mark of genius is not perfection but originality, the opening of new frontiers.

Koestler, Arthur

To the old, the new is usually bad news.

Eric Hoffer

Many of our greatest thinkers have used mental imagery to explore complex terrain and generate new possibilities. It makes sense that "image" is the root of "imagination" since picturing is central to this thought process - the use of the mind's eye to play with ideas and phenomena. To conceive of something new, we try to picture it.

Visual thinking is yet another aspect of thinking that has been neglected by too many schools or relegated to art classrooms rather than explored across the curriculum. If Newton and Einstein made powerful use of this kind of thinking, why do we see so little attention devoted to it in the science curriculum?

Perhaps we give the message that most people are condemned to memorize the imaginings of a select few, that imagination and novel thought is a rare accident of birth bestowed upon just a handful of poets, artists, scientists and philosophers whose musings the rest of us digest, commit to memory and rely upon to guide us through life. This elitist view is a self-fulfilling prophecy in too many schools. When we set such limited expectations, we are rarely surprised.

There are many effective ways to develop the power of the mind's eye and this kind of imaginative thinking. **Visual thinking** (Arnheim, 1969), a classic in the field, helped clarify the challenge and the opportunity, but since then there have dozens of programs aimed at making the sketching of ideas a basic skill, none of which have been widely adopted in schools.

Often we relegate visual thinking to the creative arts program, if we have one, and the challenge of applying such thought to social, scientific and mathematical issues for the most part sits unaddressed and unattended.

If we prize imaginative thought, we might invest in more programs to make it central to schooling and learning.

Imagine that!

4. Doubt and Wonder

While it is rarely celebrated as a major thinking skill, doubt drives some of the most productive new thought. Unquestioning loyalty to past procedures and the way things are "spozed to be" leads to blindness and paralysis. Certainty can be the enemy of both learning and innovation as old patterns and perceptions act like blinders to narrow choices and limit opportunities.

Although doubt is usually portrayed as a negative attitude, it is closely related to wondering, as we wonder how things could be different or better. Reliance upon conventional wisdom in a non-questioning manner is a recipe for disappointment.

Self doubt is an entirely different matter, as the thinker must maintain faith in the inquiry and confidence in the results. Given the frustrating and challenging nature of inquiry, the thinker must be quite resolute, capable of persisting through many periods of disappointing results.

Can we teach the young to be reasonably and responsibly skeptical regarding the world around them? Certainly. But it is a delicate matter, as Socrates discovered long ago, to show the young how they might challenge authority and conventional wisdom in a constructive and productive manner. Some sectors of the society would prefer we leave well enough alone as their power may rest on the unquestioning loyalty and obedience of the populace.

More than thirty years ago in **Teaching as a Subversive Activity**, Postman and Weingartner proposed that we equip the young with "crap detectors," the equivalent of a doubting thinking cap. Edward deBono, a more corporate source of inspiration, devotes an entire hat to critical and doubtful thinking in his **Six Thinking Hats** book. Balanced by other types of thinking, doubt plays a critically important role in identifying opportunities.

5. Consultation

Smart thinkers know how and when to check their thinking with good friends, critics, skeptics, seers and various folks who might help point out fallacies, suggest modifications and improve the end product. This skill is very difficult in practice since it requires sorting through a range of suggestions and comments, many of which may not be valuable and some of which may be quite wrong-minded. Creative thinkers must filter the suggestions, sorting and sifting, considering, reviewing and adapting incoming ideas to blend with the thinking work already started.

Many a good thinker has been seduced, distracted and unduly influenced by the ideas of others. It is difficult to invite and then manage this type of input without losing one's own voice, vision and special way of approaching the question or issue at hand.

In the early stages of one's journey, consultation may involve something like an apprenticeship. This may evolve into something more like a jam session as thinkers bounce ideas off each other. But the ultimate level of consultation engages masters of thought in an exchange that can be intense, intimidating and overwhelming even as it may prove illuminating.

This learning process may begin in school if teachers establish communities of thinkers within their classrooms, equipping all students with the group skills to support each other in reflecting about their work on thinking and questioning.

6. Extension, Refinement, Elaboration

Starting with what they know and the ideas they have at hand, thinkers can push them toward their limits, using a half dozen techniques to amplify, exaggerate, stretch, bend, distort, twist, blur or sharpen the concept, theory or model under consideration.

The process is akin to the refinement applied by a jazz musician playing around with a melody - variations on a theme. He or she might shift the amount of vibrato, the volume, the tone or the color of the music when it is time for a solo.

It might be a matter of filling in what is missing, fleshing out what was just a sketch or a skeleton of an idea. Perhaps the thinker needs to polish or sharpen the idea, eliminating rough edges and making sure the elements mesh in a supportive, coherent manner.

7. Testing

A thinker may learn the strengths or weaknesses of an idea or theory by dropping it into a realistic context to see how it fares. Hypothesis testing. Does the theory capture reality? Does the idea stand up to scrutiny? Is it mere abstraction or is it cutting edge? Will the idea draw blood? Cut a swathe? Can it take flight? Start a fire? Stay lit?

Some thinkers have a tough time coming up with ideas that are practical and sustainable. Pipe dreams and pie in the sky have their place in the creative process, but ideas must prove themselves in real terms. The testing process might disprove and dismiss the idea, but it might also point out weaknesses or fallacies that can be corrected and adjusted, thus actually strengthening the idea and adding to its value.

In some sectors of the society, this shaping of ideas is called prototyping as successive versions are tested, modified and tested again until the end result can function effectively within whatever context is intended. In this view, ideas are much like products moving from imagination to the market place.

An advertising firm has several strategies in mind for the launch of a new product. Rather than throw all their funds behind one idea, they test all three in the market with small samples. Their favorite before this test fails dramatically, so they bring in a focus group to figure out why. They learn they had offended many people by their use of slang and bad language. This they can correct.

The test saves them from embarrassment and financial loss. They can shift course, make changes and improve the product. Moving from theory into practice requires just such grounding in reality. Ideas in the abstract run the risk of still birth if they are rushed into the world too soon.

8. Tension, Reversal & Juxtaposition

Contrast and comparison provoke thought, just as incongruity raises an eyebrow and causes one to reconsider.

Dissonance creates the energy to consider different ways of thinking and to break away from the restraints of standard patterns, beliefs and procedures. The contrast, conflict and tension provoke originality.

In musical theory and composition, counterpoint is a device to develop ideas that are more complex and intriguing than simple melodies as one or more notes are played off against each other in various combinations and patterns. Note discussion from Wikipedia, the free encyclopedia, at http://en.wikipedia.org/wiki/Counterpoint.

Thinkers seek conflict and contention as a stimulant and inspiration. Like the musical composer, they intentionally set up counterpoint, hoping that the resulting "mind storms," as Pappert called them in his book of that title, will stimulate their thought and lead them to important new discoveries.

Timothy M. Melchior explains how his school district invented a model of thinking that they call "Counterpoint thinking" in his article, "Counterpoint thinking: Connecting Learning and thinking in Schools," available at http://www.chss.montclair.edu/inquiry/spr95/melchior.html.

Presented with one of ten counterpoints such as Inhumanity/Sensitivity, the students learn to avoid false dichotomies and tolerate ambiguity.

Melchior concludes . . .

"We believe that the concept of the Counterpoints helps our students to become less impulsive and more reflective, more tolerant of ambiguity and less certain, and more open and more flexible in their thinking and less categorical in their judgments. In addition, we try to teach students to resist what we call the certainty principle and the hardening of the categories, to be open to problems, new ideas, and new challenges. Most importantly, we try to teach our students that confusion is not something to be abhorred and that it can be an opportunity for growth."

In this case, juxtaposition and contrast are employed to deepen students' understanding of complexity and to stave off their rush toward premature resolution.

The thinker must learn to hold things in the balance rather than collapse into the soft center or fall for the false dichotomy.

9. Preparation & Grounding

Ironically, the thinker must usually acquire a solid foundation in the thinking of the sages, the theories of the experts and the beliefs of the academy in order to build something new and worthwhile. Invention rarely thrives on ignorance. Breakaway thinking needs a wall of ideas to push off against.

In the world of jazz, young performers must master a repertory of chord progressions and harmonies so that they can count on them as structures around which and through which they might weave more magical variations.

Schools may do a good job of introducing young folks to conventional wisdom but they do not always help with the challenging part. Hence the expression, "another brick in the wall." Thinkers cannot rely upon these institutionalized cram courses in what some call cultural literacy, however, because those who select the nuggets often bring bias and various agendas to the selection process that might leave the young person filled but not satisfied. They must learn to identify what it is that they do not know that they ought to know, to fill in the gaps and figure out what is missing.

Thinkers learn to do exhaustive literature searches so they can give due consideration to the best (and worst) thinking that has been done on the issue at hand.

10. Play, Experimentation & Improvisation

Original   Twirl   Pointilize   Wind Blast

The thinker brings a toying spirit to the challenge of exploring and inventing, testing out a wide variety of changes and variations "just for the fun of it." The use of filters in an image editing program such as PhotoShop is a good metaphor for this type of experimentation. The user may apply dozens of changes to an image and then adjust each of those changes to a level that might be appealing.

The same playful manipulation can also be done with an idea or a melody.

It is a bit difficult to demonstrate this process impressively on the pages of this book, given the conversion of a color shot into black and white for printing purposes, but a few versions of a light house should serve to make the point. The number of choices and combinations of choices is nearly unlimited for the user of PhotoShop and the same can be said for the thinker, as many of the changes made to visual images can be made to ideas.

PhotoShop Filter Categories

Artistic filters	Blur filters
Brush Stroke filters	Distort filters
Noise filters	Pixelate filters
Render filters	Sharpen filters
Sketch filters	Stylize filters
Texture filters	Video filters
Other filters	Digimarc filters
Lighting Effects filter	

Each category offers about a dozen options.
In the case of artistic filters, for example, there are fifteen choices.

Colored Pencil	Cutout
Dry Brush	Film Grain
Fresco	Neon Glow
Paint Daubs	Palette Knife
Plastic Wrap	Poster Edges
Rough Pastels	Smudge Stick
Sponge	Underpainting
Watercolor	

There are other menus offering dozens of other adjustments and changes, many of which have counterparts when making changes in music and ideas whether it be tone or contrast, intensity or hue.

Playing with such changes requires a combination of skill and attitude. The thinker must be inclined to try out many variations to see the effect of each. It is important to withhold judgment. To the casual observer it might seem as if this idea play is nothing more than diddling or fiddling about, flirting with ideas rather than constructing them in serious ways, but the process is central to inventive thought.

Often, the mind performs some of this playful manipulation at a subconscious level as ideas incubate in between more conscious thinking times. Thus, we find some of the most startling new insights suddenly pop to the surface during a morning run or a walk along a stream. Such a startling insight is often called an "Aha."

But thinkers should be able to conduct such idea play on a conscious level as well, employing a wide array of strategies like those built into PhotoShop to toy around with ideas until inspiration emerges.

11. Purposeful Wandering

New ideas often surface when the thinker can change contexts and move laterally, as Edward de Bono would put it, exploring possibilities with a fresh view. "Getting out of the box," another de Bono expression for this process, enriches the chances of novelty and invention. We are all prisoners, to some extent, of the organizations and cultures we inhabit. These social environments may shape much of our thinking in ways that are subtle so that sometimes we are unaware of their influence.

When thinkers elect to take an excursion, they are hoping that the change will do them good, that they will enjoy chance encounters with vivid and startling experiences that may refresh their thinking and awaken them to previously unthinkable prospects.

In writing this book, the author was shocked into recognizing the negative aspects of wonder, for example, during a morning run along the River Seine in Paris when the bells of Notre Dame first filled him with awe but then inspired a series of thoughts that raised the negative aspects of wonder as a tool of social control and propaganda.

One need not climb aboard a train or airplane to change context. Sometimes it is enough to stroll around the block, drive to a park or go for swim. On the other hand, more dramatic geographical and cultural shifts can often provoke more striking revelations as we are released from our normal surroundings.

12. Surrender

There are times when the thinker must relax, must suspend judgment and must open up to the flow of possibilities from outside, allowing serendipity to visit. The thinker must invite this flow. This kind of surrender is not a form of capitulation or defeat. The thinker is yielding and susceptible to the influence of unusual thoughts and thought progressions. Vulnerability, versatility and pliability combine as the thinker welcomes new directions and is actually intent on an idea altering experience. He or she is eager to experience a change of mind. The thinker is adaptable and adaptive, blending and accommodating new thoughts into the pack of pre-existing thoughts.

Relaxing and opening up in this way when wrestling with a tough thinking challenge can be most difficult, as focus and intensity seem to be essential much of the rest of the time. Relaxing seems counterintuitive. Deliberately and effectively switching gears and moods to create optimal learning and thinking conditions is not a skill set that is usually taught in any explicit manner, so young ones are apt to grow up thinking that inspiration is a mystical process that requires visits from the Muses or the use of some artificial mood enhancer such as alcohol or magic mushrooms.

The culture is full of informal expressions that touch upon this challenge as we are alternately advised to "chill out" (meaning relax and calm down) or to "get a grip." Just as confounding is the request that we "get our head around" an idea. This is a difficult task to picture or imagine.

Creating something new rarely requires mere grasping, so we might get our minds around someone else's idea, but the phrase hardly captures the birthing of new ideas. It works for understanding ideas but falls short for invention.

During the early stages of invention the thinker welcomes the arrival of new ideas and possibilities but then must become acquainted with them and consider how to fuse the new with the earlier thought. Welcoming the new is just the beginning of a complex sorting, sifting and considering process.

13. Synthesis

The thinker skillfully shifts the puzzle pieces of an idea around until a new picture emerges from the fragments. The thinker composes by moving the elements around, combining, melding, mixing and modifying them in new and different ways, It is not a simple matter of collecting, compiling and compressing. It is not mere smushing and combining or rearranging.

Unfortunately, the term synthesis is used rather freely in various state or provincial curriculum documents in ways that show little understanding of the complex process required. Too often it seems these documents really mean collecting rather than inventing. A "best evidence synthesis" is a carefully organized collection. While this type of synthesis has its place, this book will focus on more powerful types of synthesis.

The type of synthesis required for authentic thought has more to do with invention and originality than collection. It is what the thinker does with the collection that matters most, but it is this aspect of synthesis that is often neglected or ignored. Research too often stops at the collection and smushing stage.

Synthesis should serve a valuable purpose and the new composition should pass tests of quality, practicality and worth. If the team is asked to come up with an action plan to solve the problems of the Snake River, for example, it is not enough to find out what has been done in the past and smush it together into a slightly new version. This is merely "Same Old" masquerading as "New New Thing."

Such minor twisting and adjustment without depth and value is akin to the "change one word in each sentence" game played by young students trying to avoid plagiarism. Old, worn out ideas and strategies remain old and worn out if they do not match the problem-solving task at hand. The thinker must do more than come up with a plan that is new, however. Novelty does not suffice. The plan must also work.

It is easy to change the order of beads in a necklace, a perfect example of synthesis, but it is much harder to combine those beads in a more pleasing and artful manner that would stand up to some aesthetic design standards. We do not seek change for change sake. Synthesis should serve a higher purpose, some essential and striking betterment of what we know and what we have been doing.

"Rearranging the deck chairs on the Titanic" shows synthesis at its least consequential. Planners, leaders and ship captains may skirt essential issues and questions in favor of some kind of trivial pursuit that substitutes for real synthesis. In such cases we end up with virtual change rather than something worthwhile, enduring and special, or we end up with failed policies and the equivalent of ice bergs looming down on us through the fog. Planners and leaders will some times pay lip service to synthesis, creating nothing more than the illusion or change.

How does a teacher develop the questioning powers of young ones? What are the classroom moves, tactics, strategies and tricks first mentioned in Chapter 5 on quality teaching?

As with many complex tasks, the best way to learn effective questioning is by doing it under the tutelage of a master. Training will not suffice. Sustained, deep growth in skill requires a learning process more like an apprenticeship.

It is possible to provide whole class instruction in various strategies, but there is always the danger that such lessons will not stick if the learning takes place apart from authentic inquiry. Skills acquired in isolation rarely take root or become well integrated components of a thinker's repertoire.

The teacher must address two strands that operate in tandem.

The first strand is just in time instruction in specific questioning strategies, with the teacher equipping students with just what they need just as they discover they need it or just before they realize they need it. Usually this instruction occurs in the context of conducting an investigation or problem-solving activity.

The second strand is the coaching of investigative activities while they proceed. When it comes to encouraging student questioning, the teacher must move aside but not away. The teacher does much less imparting of information as activities focus on exploration and discovery. Students do the digging and the tough thinking while the teacher acts more as a consultant than an expert, supporting, guiding and helping to structure the investigation or thought process to increase productivity.

The effective teacher acquires and practices a repertoire of strategies that place primary responsibility for inquiry with the students.

A. Setting Up the Task
B. Creating a Culture and an Ethic
C. Checking on Progress
D. Intervening to Improve Results

Teaching Questioning 1

A. Setting Up the Task

Past efforts aimed at promoting what was called inquiry learning often floundered because proponents underestimated the importance of structuring the activities so that students were able to make good progress without much lost time or inefficiency. These proponents sometimes trusted too much in the natural curiosity and skills of young ones when asked to pursue issues and problems of great interest.

Many of us learned the value of scaffolding activities during those days, adding the structures, the clear directions and the pathways to produce better results. This structuring process is a matter of sound instructional design meant to replace the time-honored but discredited strategy of assigning topics and sending students to the library to "do research."

When research is nothing more than cut-and-paste collection of facts and information, little is required from teacher or student, but the challenges of more demanding research questions can lead to major frustration and failure if students are not adequately prepared or guided along the research path.

The old pathway for topical research was quite simple:

1. Go to the library.
2. Find the right encyclopedia volume.
3. Find your country.
4. Start copying words and information onto index cards.
5. Change one word in each sentence.

Little was required in the way of instructional design because the teacher did little more than assign a topic and grade the resulting paper.

Challenging questions, in contrast, require search pathways that are serpentine and complex. The research process might seem at times more like riding a roller coaster with twists, turns, dips and surprises around each corner. At other times the process might resemble a midnight walk through swampy terrain.

If a teacher expects to devote several weeks to serious research by students, it often works well to map out some of the pathways in advance. By outlining these for students, the teacher speeds them along their way.

The danger, of course, is when we do too much for students and develop dependency relationships or unduly control their thinking and exploration. We would hate to see students understanding by design just what we want them to understand. That would fulfill Pink Floyd's warning about mind control. Scaffolding and structure should ultimately drop away as young ones incorporate such structures and procedures into their natural ways of thinking, just as scaffolding is removed from a new building upon completion.

We introduce thinking structures such as graphic organizers early in the school experience with the hope that these organized ways of approaching complex challenges will become part of the students' enduring mindware. Once mastered, they form the basis for independent thought, invention and production.

When handled appropriately, scaffolding offers a number of important advantages:

- Provides clear directions
- Clarifies purpose
- Breaks down complex tasks into manageable components
- Keeps students on task
- Offers assessment to clarify expectations
- Points students toward worthy sources
- Reduces uncertainty, surprise and disappointment
- Delivers efficiency
- Creates momentum

For a full explanation of each of these features, consult "Scaffolding for Success," published in the December 1999 issue of **FNO** at http://fno.org//dec99/scaffold.html.

After decades of viewing school research as a relatively simple matter not really requiring much attention to instructional design, it is apparent that simplicity was an illusion rooted in the failure to conduct authentic research on matters of import.

Once goals are elevated to match state or provincial curriculum standards, and students are expected to wrestle with difficult questions, instructional design becomes paramount.

- Questions that require smart choices
- Questions that demand apt solutions
- Questions that call for imagination
- Questions that take a month, a year or a lifetime
- Questions that matter
- Questions that are unanswerable

Sound design of a research unit requires attention to all of the following aspects of learning:

Teaching Questioning 1

Clarification of Learning Goals - The first and most important task of all is the identification of content and process goals. In the past, content received the most attention with the emphasis upon topical research, but there was too little attention to the kinds of thinking skills that might be nurtured or the types of concepts that might be learned. By putting a greater emphasis upon thinking challenges, the unit design changes dramatically.

Consideration of Options - Once clear with regard to learning goals, the lesson designer examines a wide range of possibilities, casting aside many of the old fashioned research rituals such as hunting and gathering or trivial pursuit in favor of activities that will pay richer learning dividends. The designer considers all of the following aspects of the unit plan:

1. *Instructional Strategies* - What will the teacher do to prepare students for the tasks at hand? How will the teacher provide instructions, directions and clarification? When will the teacher step forward to direct activities and when step aside to emphasize student exploration?

2. *Learning Strategies* - How should students proceed? What pathways make sense? How can the teacher make these evident and guide students to productive inquiry? When should the teacher intervene to introduce new skills or redirect activity?

3. *Tools and Resources* - Different types of inquiries require different kinds of tools. Which make sense for the task at hand? The designer makes choices here based on value and reliability rather than fashion. If the best information resides in print resources, the unit will focus appropriately. If local rainwater must be collected to measure pH, then the choice of tools might include probes and handheld devices. If teaming is a major goal, the designer must take care to avoid saturating the class with too much equipment.

4. *Content* - The collection of information is no longer the chief purpose of the research, as information will now be synthesized and utilized to create new understandings. The designer will consider how to guide students in the process of determining which types of information will prove most

pertinent and most illuminating for the thinking task at hand.

5. *Landscape* - Because the physical arrangement of the learning space can have quite a strong influence upon the types of learning that might occur, the designer will consider how to manage that aspect of learning so as to optimize results. If teaming is valued, for example, certain kinds of tables work better than others. What are the best ways to design the layout so as to support the activities?

6. *Organization* - What are the best ways to lay out tasks so that expectations are clear and how should the work be divided or shared across members of the class? Should the teacher establish leadership or team structures? How much scaffolding is healthy?

7. *Norms* - What kinds of group attitudes and behaviors will best sustain the research effort, and how can the teacher promote or grow those attitudes and behaviors until they become characteristic, routine and enduring?

Creation of an Action Plan - While the old fashioned topical research project required little more than adherence to time-honored rituals, authentic investigations require more planning and staging of events and activities. Some of these can be done in advance, but much of this planning must evolve as the learning takes place. The twisting and often baffling turns of research demand flexibility and resourcefulness - the ability to switch gears, directions and strategies as learning occurs. The teacher sets up the basic framework of events - a skeleton suggesting activities in reasonable stages - but the students must cut their own pathways as they struggle with their questions.

Adaptation and Adjustment - Because this type of learning is full of surprises, rigid adherence to plans is counter-productive. The teacher must be quick to roll with the punches and ready to switch gears, directions and strategies as events unfold and the research progresses. There are no reliable maps and charts. Authentic research is likely to uncover much that was unanticipated and the inquiring mind will wander far from the highways of conventional thought. Path breaking is an apt analogy as the thinker must cut through thickets of underbrush and find a way through terrain rarely traveled.
The teacher could not possibly anticipate all of these surprises or

Teaching Questioning 1

prepare the class for them. In some ways it is like white water rafting on a new river without a guide or map. The rafters have no way of knowing what lies around each corner and must rely upon strength, resilience, resourcefulness and quick reflexes to match skill and strategy to challenge. They must have a repertory of skills to fit all occasions and all challenges.

The teacher can coach this process but must remain to some extent upon the sidelines or shore, allowing the young thinkers to struggle with the challenges. If the teacher pitches in and does too much paddling, the students are robbed of genuine struggle and learning.

"You might want to try X," the teachers calls out with a bull horn from the shore.

The teacher can also provide a different context, effectively changing the river or playing field on a particular day.

"Let's spend today looking at counter theories," the teacher suggests. The students put their canoes and rafts into shore and shift activities.

"Who has done work that stands in opposition to the angle you are working on? Why did they head in that direction? Were they totally crazy or did they have a clue?"

B. Creating a Culture and an Ethic

There is little in the preparation of most classroom teachers that would equip them to build collaborative communities of learners. Some teachers may have participated in professional development offerings that stress collaboration, but that is rare.

The moves, tactics, strategies and behaviors of a teacher in this classroom are quite different from those required in more didactic classrooms. These days teachers must be able to move back and forth on a spectrum between those two poles, lecturing at times with pizzazz, spirit and passion when the content requires or invites that approach but acting at other times to encourage the development of cooperative norms.

Because each class of students presents a unique challenge and is unlike any other group, the teacher must be skilled at observing the group to determine what kinds of behaviors and attitudes they show when approaching various tasks. This observation process never stops as the teacher tries to equip each student with the skills and understandings that will help them function effectively as a community of learners. The development of these attitudes and skills must proceed over many months.

Teaching Questioning 1

In most cases, the development of collaborative norms and behaviors never comes to an ideal state. Each group will struggle with its own peculiar traits and tendencies. Sometimes they will attain impressive levels of harmony and productivity, but often they will slip and slide into difficult terrain as the nature of the work can be unpredictable and far from routine. Smooth functioning thrives on routine but flounders in the face of surprise.

The teacher, then, must remain alert to these ups and downs, phases and patterns, intervening and supporting when advantageous.

Not only does the teacher work like a gardener to promote the growth of a harmonious culture, she or he also establishes an ethic, a set of beliefs about the importance of the work being done and the value of the group effort.

> What's it all about?
> Why are we here?
> Who are you?
> What is the best you can do?
> What are the important issues of life?
> What kind of thinker are you?
> What kind of group is this?

From the first hour of class, the teacher presents the class with a powerful myth and devotes the entire year to its birth and extension. The myth may take weeks before setting roots and sprouting, but it is always evident in the words and actions of the teacher.

> "This is a group that asks good questions."
> "This is a group that avoids harsh comments."
> "This is a group that persists even when the going gets frustrating."

In the first weeks of school, some of the students may find these types of statements hard to swallow, especially if their prior experience has cut in the opposite direction. Some students will actively challenge such positive norms, hoping to supplant them with more cynical, cool behaviors and attitudes.

But the teacher persists and persuades and recruits until the momentum of the group is mostly positive and the negative voices find less and less encouragement.

C. Checking on Progress

When students are exploring challenging issues and questions, the teacher watches over the process, monitoring the flow and keeping an eye on how the group is progressing. Asking students to do such work highlights the responsibility of the teacher to make sure the time is being spent productively and the students are functioning capably.

During these periods, the teacher will focus on observation and orchestration, intentionally stepping back but not away from the learning activities. As will be outlined in the next section, this watchful behavior provides the diagnostic basis for supportive interventions of various kinds.

To perform these functions well the teacher will move about from group to group and individual to individual, doing some assessment of progress through unobtrusive eavesdropping and by noticing various physical signs of focus, distraction and disruption. This movement may be supplemented by various conferencing strategies which involve calling groups or individuals to the teacher's desk or work area to discuss how the work is going.

Some teachers are concerned that a classroom focused on inquiry will become chaotic, that the students will wander off task and waste time. These concerns, along with the time-consuming nature of inquiry, serve to block some teachers from instituting this kind of learning. But the chances of chaos are minimized by the structuring mentioned earlier, especially when combined with the vigilance suggested here. When the teacher engages appropriately, the classroom will buzz with productivity.

The teacher must not stop teaching, must not abdicate responsibility for assessment and monitoring, though not all classroom teachers understand this dimension of teaching or know what the craft moves and procedures are required to make the teacher's presence an important influence on the work.

As an example of abdication, a teacher might set the students in motion and then retire to correct papers, looking up from that work only occasionally to make sure the students seem to be working quietly and well. This kind of distance does not work. The teacher must frequently come up alongside students, peer over shoulders and watch the actual work being done without too often "getting in the face" of the students. Since much of the work cannot actually be "seen" in some physical sense, the teacher must also be skilled at asking questions to uncover the work that is happening out of sight.

Teaching Questioning 1

"How is it going?'
"What are you working on now?"
"Have you encountered any frustrations?"
"What is your main strategy?"

Unfortunately, this style of teaching is poorly understood and little professional development has been provided in most places for the type of classroom management and inquiry management skills required to achieve the activity and results desired.

Enthusiasts have jokingly constrasted this approach to lecturing by calling it "The Guide on the Side" as opposed to "The Sage on the Stage," but some critics (Oppenheimer, 2003) have seized upon this simplistic notion to ridicule the movement for being some kind of lax and sloppy way of organizing learning. They watch the teacher who has moved too far to the side and rightly see that as bad teaching but they do not understand how a teacher could effectively combine structure and presence to move to the side without abdicating.

The emphasis here should be on the word "guide" as it captures the ongoing intimate engagement of the teacher with the research being conducted. Sadly, some teachers see their job narrowly as the assigning and correcting of research and do little to watch over the daily activities. In these classrooms, students are incorrectly left to their own devices and the teacher is unlikely to know if the inquiry is floundering until the work products appear. By then, it is too late to intervene.

Observation is not enough. The process is diagnostic. As the teacher notices what is happening, this awareness leads to the action decribed in the next section.

D. Intervening to Improve Results

As the teacher performs the diagnostic process outlined above, the focus moves to action.

Which of the following are appropriate for each situation?

questioning	proding	seed planting	cheering
focusing	redirecting	widening	provoking
deepening	critiquing	guiding	suggesting
directing	modeling	clarifying	validating
defining	translating	reminding	encouraging
sharpening	challenging	recommending	
moderating	disciplining	trouble-shooting	

Teaching Questioning 1

The student is more apt to learn to practice effective questioning and wondering if the teacher knows how to intervene at the right time with assistance that suppports rather than supplants the thinking of the student. It is tempting to step in heavily but that type of intervention produces little of the autonomous behavior and independence we seek to promote. The most effective intervention is likely to be a light touch, a prod, suggestion or thought provoking question that leaves primary responsibility with the student.

Knowing which light touch to apply in each case requires a blend of experience, judgment and good fortune, as the process is somewhat experimental.

During a teacher's career, it is desirable to acquire thousands of moves, tactics, tricks and strategies to promote learning.

The richer and more diverse this repertoire, the better the prospects for the teacher to match the move and tactic to the situation at hand.

The next chapter will explore futher the list of interventions shown on the previous page, providing examples of each and suggesting when they tend to be productive.

As mentioned in the previous chapter, teachers must judge carefully when to intervene and when to hold back, avoiding both interference and excessive levels of support. Managing frustration is part of the learning process for students since it is generally considered to be a basic aspect of tackling difficult issues. There are few easy answers or quick solutions. If the teacher jumps in too quickly to free students from this struggle, they will lose out on an essential learning opportunity. When the teacher does intervene, it is best to do so with the light touch mentioned earlier, selecting a few key questions to nudge the thinking and work without unduly influencing it.

During each intervention, conference or discussion, the teacher will focus on achieving one or more of three or four prime goals, encouraging students to approach their challenges in a manner that is:

- Strategic
- Reflective
- Resourceful
- Versatile

The exchanges that occur during the discussions between the teacher and the student thinkers may well be the richest source of learning new ways to question, explore and think because they are deeply rooted in actual practice. These kinds of lessons might be termed just in time teaching, as they focus on skills that are needed just then.

If the teacher steps too far away and does not engage in appropriate levels of intervention and dialogue, there is danger that students will struggle along inefficiently relying upon past practice to guide them through new thinking terrain. While some learning of new skills may occur independently from dialogue as students struggle to invent their own pathways, the amount of such independent discovery learning will vary dramatically from student to student. Some students will be caught in activity traps, spinning wheels and working industriously in ways that lead nowhere and produce no results worthy of the time invested. Some will show little evidence of the strategy, reflection, resourcefulness, flexibility and versatility mentioned above.

The effective teacher will take note of these trends within the class and will take steps to assist where and when such intervention will be most generative. In the fullest sense this means that a few words or questions might provoke several hours or days of productive work before another intervention might be required.

The teacher learns when and how to make a move.

Strategic Behaviors

As students move through their years of schooling we expect them to become increasingly astute about the choices they make when approaching inquiry tasks. Given dozens of options, we expect young ones to weigh the advantages of each approach or tactic and employ those that will be most advantageous. When they are in the early years of schooling, those options will be far more limited than later, but even in the early grades, the teacher can ask repeatedly, "What are you trying to do and how are you trying to accomplish that goal?" While there will always be some stumbling as well as trial and error when doing this kind of research, we remind students often of the need to consider choices.

"What are your choices here? What else could you do?"

To illustrate this process, consider a student busily copying down hundreds of words about a particular ship captain. The research task involves comparing the fairness of three captains when dealing with native populations encountered during Pacific voyages. The teacher watches the copying, reads some of the text and notes that much of the material seems irrelevant to the issue at hand - fairness. In a warm and encouraging manner the teacher may point to some of the notes and ask the student, "Help me understand how this information relates to fairness, Henry."

The student had lost focus and forgotten to collect only information that is pertinent, stories that provide evidence of fair actions or unfair actions. While industrious, the student had been spinning wheels and accomplishing little of value. Asked to stop and assess the import of information gathered, he must consider whether his notes cast light on the issue of fairness or not.

"Oh," he comments, waking to the challenge. "I'm not sure these stories have anything to do with fairness. They just tell about meals they shared and ceremonies they enjoyed together."

"What kinds of stories do you think you need to find, then?"

Teaching Questioning 2

This gives Henry pause to reconsider strategies.

"How about you think about that for a while and call me back when you have an idea?"

Henry is a middle school student who struggles with the teacher's question for five minutes but is stumped. He does not get it. He cannot isolate the types of stories he needs to gather because he is still unclear about evidence and clue gathering.

"I just don't know," he confesses.

The teacher sits down and asks him to recall previous class discussions of fairness with regard to the treatment of crew members by captains.

"Do you remember how we collected stories about fairness and the crew members?"

Henry nods.

"What did most of those stories have in common?"

Henry thinks for a while and then a light seems to go on.

"When a crew member did something wrong?"

The teacher nods encouragingly. "Go on . . ."

Henry smiles as the process is beginning to make sense. He thinks back to the class discussions.

"And then there were times they were short on food."

Now the teacher smiles. "So how can you use that to help you think about his treatment of the native people?"

Henry is suddenly less certain. "Well," he stumbles, "Maybe I could look to see how the captain acted when the native people did something that bothered him?"

"Like what?"

Henry is searching through his memory of stories. Suddenly his face lights up.

"Like sometimes they might take something."

"And then . . . "

"He might take someone hostage until they returned the stuff."

"And what does that tell you about fairness?"

Even a young researcher must sometimes steer through waters that may be uncharted and conditions that are quite foggy. Auto pilot does not work. We must try a variety of strategies until we find one that works.

Reflective Behaviors

As they are conducting their research we expect that our students

Teaching Questioning 2

will be thinking deeply about the issues they are exploring, actually developing their understanding of those issues as they proceed. It is tempting to bury one's head in the books and the facts, hunting and gathering without much attention to the actual construction of meaning, but that leads to a kind of collecting that is not well informed by the purpose of the study.

It turns out that pondering plays a crucial role during serious thought about difficult challenges and issues, as the researcher must keep mulling over how new evidence, new stories or new data may shift the light on the questions at hand and may alter some basic perceptions.

In the case of the ship captains mentioned earlier, for example, the student may suddenly encounter stories that showed the captain at his very worst, using excessive violence in response to problems.

"What does this mean?"

"So what?"

"How should this shape my judgment of his fairness?"

For many teachers and students, pondering while researching represents a major shift from the traditional topical school research project which was mostly about gathering up information to put in various boxes. Little pondering or considering was required.

To increase the level of reflection and pondering in a group, the teacher should model the behavior in front of the class as a whole group experience until everyone knows what it means to ponder, reflect, mull over and ruminate.

In the unit on captains mentioned earlier, the teacher devoted several class discussions to stories of discipline onboard the ships before turning the students free to research the issue of fair treatment of native peoples. During the whole class discussions, the teacher could suggest before relating each story that the students ponder its significance.

"I want you to ask yourself what this story tells us about his character and his leadership? How does this story shape your perception of him? Does it change your thinking or confirm your thinking? What can we deduce, infer or conclude based on the evidence I am sharing?"

As a matter of pedagogy, the teacher must lead students through levels of development starting with these whole group exercises and then moving toward increased levels of independence.

Even very young children can be taught to ponder, reflect and ruminate.

"Was Toad acting like a good friend? What does this story tell

80

you about Toad as a friend? What can we learn about Toad?"

Pondering, reflecting and ruminating are closely tied to wonder and wondering. It is our sense of wonder, our curiosity and our wish to understand that drive our deep thinking and pondering. It is not enough to collect facts about the ship captains. We want to know more than the facts. We want to know what kind of men they were and whether they did wrong or good.

Reflecting and pondering are meant to reveal the import of a body of facts and information.

"So what?"

Once the teacher has helped all class members to understand this aspect of research as a group, the effort moves to a more individualized version of such thinking as each student or team of students begins the search for information and meaning. The teacher must use the observation and conferencing strategies mentioned earlier to promote this kind of reflective practice to guard against mere collecting.

"What new stories have you found today?"

"What do they tell you about the Captain?"

"Have these stories changed your thinking in any way?"

"What's going on in your mind today as you read and consider?"

"What are you pondering?"

Resourceful Behaviors

In order to fashion new ideas and uncover new possibilities, the student must learn to leave no stones unturned, must be willing to exhaust all possibilities, and must have the skill to exploit all avenues of investigation and thought.

Often a search will prove frustrating as the availability of pertinent information and actual evidence or facts may be quite limited. Much of the information readily available on various issues is secondary in nature, meaning that an author has studied the topic or issue enough to write an essay or some kind of summary document that may take a stand, explain the issue and provide some evidence to substantiate the author's point of view. For the student who hopes to get to bedrock, reliance upon secondary sources would be foolhardy. In many cases, the authors of such work have selected their evidence in ways that may match their point of view.

In one article about Captain Cook, for example, that has been withdrawn for correction, the author claimed that Cook set a good example of how to treat native peoples but left out of the ensuing account any mention of his hostage taking or other brutal actions.

We would hardly want to applaud Captain Cook for his hostage taking or brutality, but a student who looks no further than this secondary source would emerge with a distorted, untruthful image of Cook that would not stand up to scrutiny once the actual stories of Cook's actions were examined. On the day he was stabbed to death by the Hawaiians, for example, he had been trying to take one of their chiefs hostage because a long boat had been stolen. The Hawaiians in that instance at least did not share the above author's judgment of Cook and were apparently angry enough to end his career.

The resourceful student, then, leaves no stone unturned and seeks out evidence that is substantial and reliable rather gliding along on the easy pickings of secondary sources.

Teachers can promote this kind of resourceful behavior in much the same way they can promote reflection. They begin with large group sessions during which a passage like the one above is employed to raise the issue of the reliability of primary sources and secondary sources. Students walk through an investigation as a large group noting the difference between unsubstantiated opinions and concrete evidence. Faced with weak material and limited resources, they are challenged to figure out where else they might look.

"How are we going to find out what Cook did?"

"If we cannot find many stories of what he did on the Net, then where else can we look?"

"Where do you suppose the stories are?"

This kind of class discussion prepares students for the day when they will be operating independently and facing similar frustrations. While some educators speak glowingly of fertile questions and investigations, the search is often quite baffling. The question may end up arid rather than fertile. The path to understanding may prove Byzantine or labyrinthine. The availability of pertinent evidence may be elusive. The quest may be plagued by cul de sacs, false leads and the intellectual equivalent of fool's gold, but we expect our students to persist and prove themselves adept at finding what they need.

Again the teacher turns to observation and dialogue:

"How are you doing today?"
"Are you finding what you need?"
"Where have you looked so far?"
"What else do you have in mind?"

Teaching Questioning 2

Versatile Behaviors

Exploration of complex issues and challenges requires both flexibility and ingenuity. The thinker cannot rely upon recipes, formulas or set pathways. The search often involves invention. The clever reporter and the cagey detective know how to shift directions and try out many different approaches and techniques. They may dig, dart, weave or backtrack according to the demands of the moment, but they rarely put their heads down and charge blindly ahead without looking.

Charging right ahead is not uncommon when many people seek answers, but it is rarely effective. Teachers can alert students to the dangers of plowing right ahead and can demonstrate the value of versatility.

The ending of the old saying, "If at first you don't succeed," needs to be changed to "Try a different approach."

As with the other behaviors advanced in this chapter, the teacher can introduce and model versatility in large group sessions until it is well understood by all the students.

The teacher might, for example, conduct a series of Google searches with all of the students watching.

Looking for evidence of his fairness or unfairness to members of his crew, the teacher might start in the Advanced version of Google and enter "Captain Cook" in the exact phrase box while trying the phrase "unfairness to members of his crew" in the top box.

This strategy would turn up little of value or note.

So the teacher would try something different and talk to the class about the process.

"Maybe I should use different words? Any suggestions?"

One member of the class suggests replacing "unfairness" with "unfair," so they give it a try. Then another student suggests using words like "treatment" or "discipline" or "flogging." The class tries out different words and phrases but also plays with the different features of the Advanced version to see how they can narrow or improve the focus of their search.

The teacher demonstrates how they can use ".edu" or ".gov" in the Domain box to limit results to Web sites that are educational or governmental.

By working together on this search students learn first hand the value of versatility and can then incorporate this approach into their own research.

Once again the teacher makes sure they are practicing versatility by combining observation and dialogue.

Teaching Questioning 2

"Are you feeling stuck?"
"Is there some other approach that might work better for you?"
"What else could you try?"

Chapter 10 - Essential Questions

These are questions that touch our hearts and souls. They are central to our lives. They help to define what it means to be human. Most of the important thought we will conduct during our lives will center on such *essential questions*.

- What does it mean to be a good friend?
- What kind of friend shall I be?
- Who will I include in my circle of friends?
- How shall I treat my friends?
- How do I cope with the loss of a friend?
- What can I learn about friends and friendships from the novels we read in school?
- How can I be a better friend?

When we draw a cluster diagram of the *Questioning Toolkit* as we did in Chapter Four of this book, essential questions stand at the center of all the other types of questions. The other question types serve the purpose of "casting light upon" or illuminating one or more Essential Question.

The term was first introduced by Grant Wiggins and the Coalition of Essential Schools in the 1980s. (Cushman, 1989) Since that time, the term has spread widely into models for the design of curriculum and lessons.

Most essential questions are interdisciplinary in nature. They usually cut across lines created by schools and scholars to mark the terrain of departments and disciplines. Essential questions usually probe the deep and often confounding issues confronting us - complex and baffling matters that elude simple answers:

Life - Death - Marriage - Identity - Purpose - Betrayal - Honor - Integrity - Courage - Temptation - Faith - Leadership - Addiction - Invention - Inspiration.

They pass the test of "So what?"

They focus on matters of import.

Essential Questions

The greatest novels, the greatest plays, the greatest songs and the greatest paintings all explore essential questions in some manner. Essential questions are at the heart of a search for Truth.

Many of us believe that schools should devote more time to essential questions and less time to *Trivial Pursuit*.

What are the traits of an essential question?

- The question probes a matter of considerable importance.
- The question requires movement beyond understanding and studying - some kind of action or resolve - pointing toward the settlement of a challenge, the making of a choice or the forming of a decision.
- The question cannot be answered by a quick and simple "yes" or "no" answer.
- The question probably endures, shifts and evolves with time and changing conditions - offering a moving target in some respects.
- The question may be unanswerable in the ultimate sense.
- The question may frustrate the researcher, may prove arid rather than fertile and may evade the quest for clarity and understanding.

Unfortunately, the term is often bandied about with little rigor, definition or clarity so that many pedestrian and insignificant questions slip in under the term simply because they are large, sweeping and grand in some respects. Essential questions are not simply BIG questions covering lots of ground.

To trace the decline and fall of the Roman Empire is a grand task, an enormous task, but it hardly makes for an essential question because it lacks focus and fails to move past description to analysis, synthesis or evaluation.

If we were to ask instead how our modern state, be it Australia, the United States or Canada, might avoid a decline like the one experienced by the Roman Empire, we would convert mere collecting and description into a much more important and intriguing task.

It is not the sweep or the grandeur of the question that matters so much as the significance of the issues addressed. Matters of import are the crux of the matter.

Sven Birkerts identifies this challenge in a selection from his **Gutenberg Elegies** (1995):

Essential Questions

> Resonance — there is no wisdom without it. Resonance is a natural phenomenon, the shadow of import alongside the body of fact, and it cannot flourish except in deep time.
>
> **Page 75**

Essential questions explore matters of import. They are worthy of our time and are likely to spark interest and awaken curiosity. They require new thought rather than the mere collection of facts, second hand opinions or cut-and-paste thinking.

We can convert traditional school questions into essential questions using a strategy fully outlined in Chapter 22 of this book.

The chapter proposes ten question functions to focus the transformation process:

Build or Invent	Challenge or Destroy
Decide	Figure Out
Persuade or Convince	Wonder
Acquaint	Dismiss
Predict	Understand

For each of these question functions, the chapter defines the function and then provides examples of traditional school questions being upgraded to a higher level of significance.

In the case of the Understanding function, for example . . .

Understand

In popular terms, the goal of this questioning activity is to "get one's head around" some topic, idea, challenge or proposal. By the end, one hopes to grasp key traits, elements and structures.

Traditional School Question

Go find out about Robert or Elizabeth Browning (or any other poet, general, prime minister, hero, character, celebrity, scoundrel or seer. What did he or she do?

Upgraded Version
What were the five most distinguishing characteristics of

Essential Questions

Browning and how did they contribute to her success of failure? What made her great or not so great? What are the two or three most important things you learned about her that might serve you well?

The chapter will serve as a valuable resource for any teacher wishing to reexamine and redesign classroom inquiry activities to require a higher level of thought.

Examples of Essential Questions

In schools, essential questions may offer the organizing focus for a single discussion, a month's unit of study or a whole year's exploration. Outside of school, of course, essential questions might challenge us for years. We may struggle with questions of a lifetime as well as questions of the day. We may have close and brief encounters with monumental issues or longstanding relationships with queries that dog us, defy us or delight us. We cannot nail down essential questions in simple time frames.

In this section we will look at school examples that work well at four age levels:

- Primary Grades - Students from the age of 4 to 8.
- Intermediate Grades - Students from the age of 9-12.
- Middle School - Students from the age of 13-15.
- High School - Students from the age of 16-18.

Primary Grades

Questions about traits are especially powerful for this age group as young ones try to understand the world around them.

- What are the traits of a good fast food restaurant?
- What makes a good friend?
- What makes a good town?
- What makes a good day?
- What makes a bad storm?
- How can we be safe?
- How can we eat well?
- What kind of TV programs are healthy for us?
- What kinds of cereals are healthy for us?

Essential Questions

Traits are at the heart of evaluation on **Bloom's Taxonomy** - the skill of making wise choices based on criteria and evidence. Traits are the basis for the values and criteria that drive choices.

Another major strategy to introduce young students to essential questions is to focus on questions requiring analysis. Such questions play to the natural curiosity and wonder of children seeking to figure things out and understand how things work.

• Why do you suppose the rain falls down?
• Why do you suppose some birds fly south in the winter?
• Why do you suppose the boy in this story cheated?
• Why do you suppose the girl in this story lied?
• Why do you suppose some people break their promises?

Primary students are also ready for flights of fancy, questions that invite them to speculate, predict, invent or imagine.

• What do suppose would happen if we took away all television?
• If it snows heavily this winter, how will that make life different?
• If you could change the town we live in, how would you make it better?
• If you were asked to design a new playground for the school, how would you do it?
• If you were the boy in this story, how would you handle the problem he faces?
• If you were the woman in this story, how would you change things to make them better?

Intermediate Grades

The types of questions mentioned above work well for this age group, but the complexity and depth may change to match the growing reasoning capacity of the students.

Traits remain a potent focus:

• What are the traits of a good ship captain?
• What are the traits of a good leader?
• What makes for a fair punishment?
• What makes one team better than another?
• What makes one writer more powerful than another?
• What makes one story more believable than another?

89

Essential Questions

• What makes one country more just than another?

Analysis questions are critically important as students will be called upon to figure things out and demonstrate inferential reasoning on increasingly difficult tests. Instead of finding answers, students must make answers, putting clues together to solve a mystery or build a case.

• Why do you suppose the character in this story decided to abandon his friend?
• Why do you suppose the gas in this experiment acted the way it did?
• Which behaviors shown by the main character were evidence of strong character and which ones showed weakness?

Upper elementary students also welcome questions that invite them to speculate, predict, invent or imagine.

• Are we at risk from earthquakes here?
• Is there anything our town should do to improve our readiness for natural disasters?
• Could a tsunami happen here? Are we ready? What should we do?
• How could you invent a better plan? a better city? a better ending? a better poem? a better song? a better logo? a better message? a better rule or law?

Middle School

Older students continue to work on understanding the characteristics or traits that set particular examples apart as distinguished and special.

• How do we know if a law is just?
• How do we know if a poet, a playwright or a novelist is promising?
• How is a hero different from a celebrity?
• What kinds of harm can be done by fame and fortune?

Older students can also handle complex choices which require the skill of evaluation on **Bloom's Taxonomy.**

Essential Questions

- Which of these three poets writes the most powerful and evocative poetry?
- If you were moving to China for two years, which of these six cities would you select?
- Which leader (prime minister, president, etc.) of the previous century did the most to advance the cause of civil rights and liberties?
- Which leader relied the most on propaganda, demagoguery and appeals to fear?

Understanding why life turns out the way it does is another major focus for essential questions at this age.

- Why do you suppose some people can handle being a celebrity without losing their sense of self while others slip into oblivion, drug use and other forms of self destruction?
- Why do some cities and states seem capable of overcoming terrible troubles and misfortune, rising to challenges with grace and courage while others surrender, collapse and give up the fight with a whimper?
- Why do some friends stick by you even during the worst of times while others are quick to flee at the first sign of trouble?

As with the younger students, invention and problem-solving can also inspire questioning and thinking at this middle level.

- What should be done to improve the effectiveness of the United Nations?
- How can our nation best handle the influx of immigrants?
- How can our nation best provide for security without undermining important civil liberties?
- How should the copyright laws be adjusted to take into account the impact of new technologies?
- What should be done about homelessness and poverty?
- What is the best way to balance the need for resource development with protection of the environment?
- How can the writing in this essay be improved?

High School

If students have enjoyed several years of working with challenging questions and issues prior to entering high school, the choice of

Essential Questions

essential questions will move toward depth and complexity, demanding more in the way of originality, perception and discovery.

If, on the other hand, students have had limited experience with such challenges, then many of the types of questions listed in earlier sections will be a good starting place.

At earlier grade levels it makes some sense to "chunk" the content, allowing students to wrestle with parts of much larger questions, in part because those questions might take months to explore with any degree of finality. In comparing a half dozen Chinese cities, for example, students might come away with a firm grasp of the comparative thought process by looking at nothing more than the weather, recognizing that climate is only one of a dozen or more major criteria worthy of research if one had the time.

As students reach high school, such chunking is replaced by more demanding investigations that might span weeks and even months. We expect students to experience the benefits of digging deeply. While it is easy to fall into the trap of assigning brief and superficial research projects, that practice does a disservice to the students, who should be emerging from high school with the capacity to conduct research into the most difficult of life's issues.

Employing a curricular approach called "Science, Technology and Society, the teacher begins the unit with a slide show that illustrates the impact of chemistry on the landscape, a show that provokes strong reactions from the students and serves as a hook to capture their interest.

Within the next few days, the teacher shares sample questions and encourages students to generate their own.

- What is the price of progress?
- How can we enjoy the fruits of chemistry without spoiling our world?
- What are the best examples of responsible disposal practices?
- What should the government be doing to regulate the impact of chemicals on the farms, rivers and forests of our nation?
- What changes need to be made to the Super Fund clean-up program?
- What are the most dramatic contributions made to the quality of life by chemical products?
- What are the products with the most damaging impact?

Essential Questions

How Essential Questions Interact

Essential questions provide the impetus for investigations and research. Usually there is a single essential question that is center stage. This question fuels and directs the inquiry process. All of the other questioning types act in service to the essential question, contributing whatever they can to the resolution of whatever issue, quandary, challenge or problem is presented by the essential question.

If properly stated, the essential question has a dramatic impact, evoking a passionate level of interest as well as a firm commitment to persevere until a satisfying level of understanding is reached. A good essential question provokes a dynamic tension that should persist throughout the phases of research. At no time should the researcher lose sight of the goal at hand or become so immersed in the data collection that the primary issue and question is laid aside. Because data collection is meant to cast light on the question, the collection should be done with focus and purpose, the gathering restricted to that which is pertinent, promising or illuminating.

The essential question looms over the enterprise at all times like the sun or the moon or a morning star. The prominence of other question types may shift from phase to phase as utility and value change according to the task at hand, but the essential question will remain a guiding influence at all times.

This is easy to say and easy to write but not an easy habit of mind to develop in young ones who may have experienced years of the old fashioned kind of school report that required little more than gathering. The entire notion and value of cognitive dissonance is usually foreign to students until teachers have shown them how it operates to stimulate curiosity and drive inquiry.

The essential question is a thing of wonder. It probes some aspect of life so profound that the human spirit is captivated and cannot rest until the dissonance is reduced or settled, until there is some degree of resonance and understanding.

We expect the student to keep wondering throughout the research process, weighing the relevance of each new clue, each chunk of data and each discovery to the question at hand.

The essential question becomes a preoccupation as the researcher finds the questioning process almost continuous. Many times the thinking may continue more or less unconsciously as an incubation process operating behind the scenes, but all of a sudden a thought may surface in the middle of a run or a shower or a walk along the river.

93

Reverence and wonder are closely allied. There are times in life when we should bow before beauty and grace, when we must acknowledge the power and majesty of institutions that have managed to capture and transmit something magnificent and transcendent. At their best, such organizations, whether they be a hospital, a university or a branch of the military, take us beyond the mundane and the trivial. They may inspire us to make remarkable contributions to society and rise above greed and selfishness to do good works.

Preaching irreverence, then, must seem paradoxical, but respect for these great institutions and traditions should not blind us to their shortcomings and failings. It is a matter of balance. We know that greatness can only survive and persist if each generation holds these institutions to high standards and expects them to adjust to changing conditions.

It takes courage to challenge conventional wisdom or the prevailing order, but the continuing health of any organization or institution depends upon such questioning. Autocratic nations and organizations prize unquestioning loyalty and obedience while democracy thrives on dissent and a strong dose of irreverent questions. Blind obedience isolates the organization from reality and makes corrective action difficult as truth is sacrificed on the altar of loyalty.

Irreverent questions often explore territory that is considered "off-limits" or taboo. Sadly, the recruitment process within many organizations often silences dissent and rewards compliance. The young person climbing the ladder learns that if you want to get along, you must go along. If the boss has a stupid idea, it too often pays to smile and feign adoration. Prospects for promotion are rarely enhanced by pointing out the nakedness or the folly of the leader. The sycophant advances. The Doubting Thomas languishes in the mail room. At its worst, this phenomenon breeds abuse and corruption as leaders of the church or corporation indulge in excesses of one kind or another, whether they be accounting schemes or sexual misconduct.

Irreverent questions challenge more than conventional wisdom. They test the claims of authority, institutions and myths, probing beyond the surface seeking verity and validation. Instead of taking the authority, institution or myth at face value, these questions provide a reality check. They frequently leap over, under or through walls, rules and regulations.

If we expect our young ones to learn and practice this type of questioning, we must also teach them the political survival skills to accompany what might otherwise prove to be suicidal behavior, as we have watched whistle-blowers and critics crucified rather than exalted.

Socrates was executed for encouraging the youth of Athens to ask irreverent questions. We need to remember that such questioning is not universally appreciated. Many folks find such questioning disrespectful and impolite. They doubt the value of irreverent questions. They prefer loyalty and faith.

Corporations like IBM might have learned that today's heretic - the one with the courage, the tenacity and the brash conviction to question the way things are "spozed to be" - often turns out to be a prophet of sorts. Enthralled by decades of success, such organizations often cruise along on yesterday's truths even as conditions change and those truths lose merit. The organization's dogma may become self defeating as true believers ignore the signs that the times are changing.

Because IBM was slow to listen to those questioning time-honored practices and mind sets, it nearly died during the late 1980s. Suddenly gasping for survival, it laid off tens of thousands of employees, brought in dramatically different leadership and re-invented itself, lurching and stumbling into a new business model that was long overdue. Wedded to a set of strategies and rituals that had served well for decades, the organization was unable to shift behaviors and beliefs until it became a matter of survival.

The Emperor's New Clothes is a classic story showing what happens when irreverent questions are discouraged while obedience, subservience and compliance are prized. The emperor parades naked. The corporation clings blindly to old beliefs. The tailors make fortunes selling fraudulent goods. It takes a boy's simple questions to produce End Game. The rest of the world has been going along to get along.

It is the rare school that sets the goal of teaching young ones to question authority. Sadly, the opposite is more often the case. Schools often prize compliance and unquestioning fealty. Thus we have Pink Floyd's "Another brick in the wall" and charges of mind control.

Can we teach young ones to balance respect and irreverence?

It seems essential during times of change. If we expect organizations and institutions to adjust and adapt, they will need employees who can think in this manner, respecting traditions and history while considering the potential for new ways of doing things.

Schools need to formally acknowledge the value of such thinking

Irreverent Questions

and provide students with opportunities to practice such questioning. At the same time, they must take care to avoid breeding cynicism and despair.

Examples of Irreverent Questions

Because schools may be somewhat reluctant to engage students in too much controversial material, the thought process required to pursue irreverent questions can be learned by avoiding one's own backyard and studying the institutions of those who are far distant in time or geography.

Rather than repeating the mistakes of the past, we hope this generation will learn from those mistakes and will ask tough questions of the kings, the politicians and the movers and shakers of previous centuries. They can also apply this questioning skill to institutions or governments that are far away.

When they come of age they will be prepared to employ such questioning to improve their community and their place of work.

Primary Grades

Fiction provides an excellent source for this kind of questioning as stories often show animals or people in community settings or kingdoms. Many of these communities or kingdoms are suffering from a bad ruler or bad rules. The fiction may raise essential issues of fairness. A character may act like the boy in the story of the Emperor's New Clothes. Students can learn about irreverent questions by reading stories that show them in action.

- Why do you suppose Sam was so unhappy about the club?
- What seemed wrong about the club's rules?
- What would you ask the club leader if you wanted her to reconsider the rules?
- What other questions do you think a club should ask about its rules?
- Did Sam do a good job of raising questions about fairness?

Intermediate Grades

Along with a continuing use of fiction in the manner outlined above, intermediate grades can use news reports and periodicals to explore current events and issues. We look for stories of institutional and organizational excesses or failures.

- What do you think went wrong in this company?
- How do you think they got in so deep before anyone complained?
- What do you think the employees should have done?
- If you had worked in this company and saw what was happening, what kinds of questions would you have raised?
- Of whom would you have asked these questions?
- Do you think this would have helped?
- Did any of the employees try raising questions?
- What was their fate?
- What can you learn from them?

Middle School

Students at this level can explore more complex issues and will often welcome this type of questioning as early adolescents are eager to challenge authority and wonder about these issues whether we encourage it or not. At the same time, they can be prone to a level of disengagement, disenchantment and disinterest regarding adult institutions, rituals and patterns that can undercut serious consideration of how these might be improved.

- Since technologies are changing the music business in dramatic ways, why do you suppose some companies have been so slow to adjust their policies?
- If you worked for a record company five years ago, what questions do you think you should have been asking top management to consider?
- If you had asked them, what do you suppose would have been your reward or fate?
- Are there any companies that made this transition well?
- How do suppose Apple Computer was able to change its approach to music so dramatically?
- What questions were critical in helping them to change their business strategies?

Both biography and fiction can provide students at this level and on into high school with compelling stories of people who rocked the boat, challenged the prevailing order and risked their lives or careers to try to bring about change. Some of these characters and figures are now portrayed as heroes. Others are seen as villains or traitors, depending on one's values and point of view. We encourage students to read these stories so they might develop a personal code of conduct that might guide their own choices in the future. Working for an Enron or a Martha Stewart or a Donald Trump, what questions will they ask, if any, and how will they deal with ethical issues as they become employees?

High School

By the time students enter high school, many have already started working and are beginning to struggle with issues they notice in the community. We continue to provide them with models of thoughtful dissent, but we also want them to consider cases where the challenger really was a heretic motivated by less than admirable purposes. We hope they can distinguish between responsible and irresponsible questioning.

- How would you characterize the relationship between Thomas Moore and his king?
- Do you think Moore was a hero, a martyr, a traitor or a heretic?
- What questions did Moore ask?
- Which of these probably angered the King the most?
- Would you have asked those same questions if you were Moore?
- When is it better to remain silent? Is it ever better?
- What made Moore do what he did?

At this age many students can grapple with problems-based learning projects where they gather data, diagnose a problem and create an action plan to generate corrective action. These may involve irreverent questions during both the opening and the final stages of the project, as students begin by asking what might possibly be wrong and conclude by asking how they might motivate the governing institutions to take action.

- Is the river passing through town healthy?
- Can I drink its water without treatment?
- Can I swim in the river safe from infection?
- What are the prime risks to the river?
- What agencies are responsible for the river's health?
- Are they doing the responsible thing?
- What is the responsible thing?
- What are the most important ways we need to improve the

river's health?
- Once we know what action is needed, how can we motivate the responsible agencies to embrace our suggestions?
- Why aren't they doing this questioning themselves?

How Irreverent Questions Interact with Others

Irreverent questions are usually connected to an essential question that involves problem-solving as described in the section on the river above. To come up with a program of action, the researcher must conduct a needs assessment. In many cases, the establishment may be invested in supporting or maintaining the current state of affairs. They may suffer from denial or they may simply prefer to keep things as they are. The irreverent question is likely to operate in a series as the researcher explores avenues of opportunity, trying to figure out just what is happening and what needs to be done.

Probing questions translate irreverent questions into scalpels, drills and bits as the researcher tries to gather specific evidence to validate the more general concern identified by the irreverent question.

The irreverent question might be, "Is this candidate as virtuous as he would like us to believe?" Probing questions might be, "What was he doing on that boat last weekend?" or "Has he accepted any favors from those doing business with the state or the city?"

Chapter 12 - Irrelevant Questions

Ignorance is bliss, so they say.
Really? Who says?
Bliss it might be until the sky falls!
Sadly, we are often blind-sided by the unexpected. We are caught off guard and unsuspecting.
In an age when terrorists specialize in doing the unthinkable, we must learn to think the unthinkable and ask the seemingly irrelevant question.
"How do we protect our middle school from a terrorist attack?"
This was a seemingly irrelevant question until the first week of September, 2004, when Chechen rebels took an entire school hostage and hundreds (338+) were slaughtered.
Is it still an irrelevant question? For them? For us?
If we could learn to ask apparently irrelevant questions during the planning process, we might create a plan to meet the unsuspected.
What's the worst that could happen?
Good question - one probing apparently irrelevant domains.

What do we need to know?
What don't we know we don't know?

This photo of Rodin's Thinker is the obvious, clichéd, frontal view. Visitors repeatedly capture the face or the side view. Few step around and show the back, the straining torso, the rear view.

Much thinking proceeds with the same limited perspective and limited view of reality. One must learn to step around and consider all the angles.
Can we establish habits of mind that tilt toward the unusual perspective, reward walking about and looking askance?
Is he pondering?

Irrelevant Questions

Is he wondering what he needs to know?
Is Rodin's Thinker stuck?
Or is he capable of what deBono would call "lateral thinking" -
the ability to step out of the box of conventional wisdom to consider
fresh possibilities?

When we don't know what we don't know . . .
It is quite difficult to explore the unknown, in part because it is off
the radar and out of sight.
"Out of sight is out of mind."
But the most promising mental territory may be that uncovered by
the seemingly irrelevant question.
The irrelevant question is a peculiar member of the *Questioning
Toolkit*. Its power is counter-intuitive and its practice is rare.
One must learn to escape from the limitations of conventional
wisdom and thinking by ranging farther afield. In fact, this kind of
exploration requires dramatic excursions into unfamiliar terrain.
One learns to walk around the statue . . .
Truth rarely appears where we might look logically. The creation
of new knowledge almost always requires some wandering off course.
The more we cling to coastline, the less apt we are to find the New
World. As Melville so dramatically pointed out in **Moby Dick**, the
search for truth requires the courage to venture out and away from the
familiar and the known. In his chapter on the Lee Shore, Melville
comments . . .

But as in landlessness alone resides
the highest truth, shoreless, indefinite
as God—so, better is it to perish in
that howling infinite, than be inglori-
ously dashed upon the lee, even if
that were safety!

Exploring the Dark Side

Artists frequently employ the concept
of negative space to capture the shape of
space surrounding an object.
The same concept works well to
identify the missing parts of a mental
puzzle.
We try to extend our search beyond

Irrelevant Questions

the boundaries of what we already know. We aim our searchlight into the shadows and the dark places.

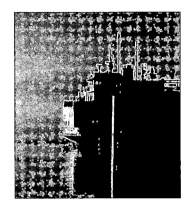

We cast light into corners, under bushes, into closets, and through locked doors and barriers.

How do we build a bridge from what we know to what we need to know? What strategies allow us to penetrate the fog, sailing through darkness to emerge with increased understanding?

How do we achieve illumination?

How do we shed preconceptions, bias and false certainties?

How can we create a map of regions never explored?

Can we figure out what it is we do not know?

Strategy One - The Jigsaw Puzzle, Juxtaposition, and Worst Case Scenarios

We can use the jigsaw puzzle as a metaphor for this kind of thinking. Faced with a pile of a thousand landscape pieces, we hardly know where to begin, but after we gather edges and begin to fill in a few sections, what is missing begins taking form in contrast to what is found.

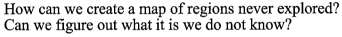

Extend this metaphor to a cluster diagram. First we map what we know on the left side of a cluster diagram.

We then create a matching set of empty boxes on the right as unknowns.

103

Irrelevant Questions

Making plans without paying attention to what might possibly go wrong is dangerous - the equivalent of wishful thinking.

Using the juxtaposition strategy, the diagram would be augmented to force consideration of disappointments and obstacles. The two columns on the right ask important questions.

* What could go wrong? * What have we overlooked?

Anticipating problems, obstacles and hurdles strengthens the planning process and reduces the chances of failure.

The same planning process works well when bringing new technologies into schools, when hoping to transform the reading program of a school or when asking what steps need to be taken to increase homeland security.

Some planners call this process scenario-building. The goal is to spin out an array of situations that might arise despite our best hopes and efforts - scenarios ranging from optimistic and provident to disastrous. Smart planners include at least one "worst case scenario" in their preparations so that they have strategies in mind to protect them against the dark side of life. We would expect our students to learn such strategies early in life to protect them from folly later in life.

Strategy Two - Reversal

We purposefully turn an issue, problem or challenge upside down and inside out. We take the issue, problem or challenge and spin it about to look at all the different angles. If black, look at the white or blue.

Planning to install a new reading program? Consider removal of a reading program, a step usually overlooked when introducing some-

Irrelevant Questions

thing new. Introducing an after school program? Consider a morning substitute. Trying to cut down on the incidence of antisocial behaviors? Give thought to increasing the frequency of good deeds and good works.

While each of these are a matter of words, semantics and emphasis, these mental frameworks can have a deciding impact on the way a challenge is approached and change is made.

Strategy Three - Grab the Tail

When caught on the horns of a dilemma, grab the tail!

Classic problem-solving strategies abound for those who are stuck in their planning. In all too many cases, we fixate on a few options and fail to invest adequately in spinning out options. We narrow choices too rapidly and then agonize over the resulting scarcity of possibilities. Many organizations rush to deal with symptoms of problems rather than root causes. Later they lament the failure of policy. Edward deBono preaches lateral thinking and out-of-the-box thinking as a way to capture the process of generating a richer array of choices. Likewise, Roger von Oech writes of unlocking mental locks that stand in the way of generating imaginative and novel solutions.

The folk wisdom of grabbing the tail captures the essence of both.

Strategy Four - Purposeful Wandering - Learning to Get Lost!

Once we accept that we may not know what we do not know, the notion of getting lost takes on new meaning. We hope to leave our biases, our presumptions, our ignorance and our limitations behind as we step over the boundary lines and launch a voyage of discovery and exploration. We leave our comfort zone and strike out for parts unknown. We escape narrow, provincial thinking and open our minds to the full range of human possibilities. We set ideology behind and give full consideration to what might be true.

Hundreds of years ago, the journey might have been by canoe or sailing vessel. The explorers ventured into uncharted waters.

Today it might be more a matter of exploring ideas. Sometimes we can take advantage of digital tools to expand our understanding.

A thesaurus will point out linkages and associations we might not have anticipated, for example. The Visual Thesaurus at http://www.visualthesaurus.com provides a particularly vivid example of this exploration process. The visitor to this site follows trails and linkages that evolve like pathways through a magic forest.

Search engines may also support purposeful wandering in powerful ways. TEOMA.com provides linkages and associated search options that the user might not have considered.

Look up the term "discovery" on TEOMA and along with the usual list of web pages, it will suggest other searches:

- Data Mining
- Discovery Channel
- Drug Discovery
- Text Mining
- Clark Expedition
- Resource Discovery

Programs like these help thinkers to tap into resources they might not have otherwise considered.

Strategy Five - Theater of the Absurd and Beyond the Pale

While it would be nice if the world, human behavior and the nature of life were all logical, reasonable and sensible, much is irrational and very strange. Logical and sensible people sometimes have difficulty thinking illogically, so they are limited in their ability to contend with illogical forces, extremists and highly emotional opponents.

Playwrights like Samuel Beckett, Eugene Ionesco, Jean Genet and Harold Pinter coined the term "Theater of the Absurd" in the 1950s.

Planners who limit their thinking and their reading to like-minded thinkers and planners are unlikely to understand the thinking of irrational opponents, insurgents, seers, prophets and demagogues. Unpleasant as it might seem, we must all extend our reading, our listening and our thinking to penetrate the veils and walls surrounding the dreams, wishes, lies, plans and strategies of those who live, think, operate and act beyond the pale.

If we never read what dissidents and radicals are writing and thinking, we are likely to wake up to unthinkable headlines when they take actions that seem horrific. If we surround ourselves with true believers of our own faith, we may make very poor chess players when face to face with those of different persuasions.

To avoid horrific surprises, we must extend our definitions of

Irrelevant Questions

intelligence to include the search for the radical, the absurd and the illogical. Rather than suppressing all media that lie beyond the pale, we might sometimes pay attention to some of the laments, the threats and the rallying cries.

Counter insurgency without deep knowledge of an opponent is a good example of theater of the absurd posing as rational policy.

Strategy Six - Taking Soundings and Mapping the Unknown

Long before Captain James Cook appeared on the scene, Pacific islanders had been sailing hundreds of miles of open ocean between islands using quite complicated navigational systems to find their way. Relying upon constellations, currents and many natural clues, they were able to travel far and still find their way home.

Captain Cook devoted much of his career to carefully charting on paper those regions of the world that had not yet been charted (in European terms). With his collection of charts drawn by other European explorers and the help of Pacific Islanders, he set about filling in the missing regions by sailing into them to see if there were land forms worthy of charting.

When sailing into a harbor unknown to Europeans, a member of his crew routinely used a lead to take soundings (judge the depth of the water). These were added to the chart as one more measure of the world being described.

The construction of knowledge and especially the discovery of new ideas and possibilities must also proceed by venturing, sounding and mapping.

Examples of Irrelevant Questions

Primary Grades

At this age, young ones can learn to ask seemingly irrelevant questions when planning for a field trip or a class event such as a party. Planning of any kind is a fertile practice field for such questioning.

- What should we bring on the trip?
- What kinds of questions should we be asking about the weather?
- What kinds of things should we be learning before we actually visit the museum?

107

Irrelevant Questions

- Could we end up too hot? too cold? wet?
- Could we get hungry? be bored?
- Could we get lost and be separated from the group?
- Could we be approached by a stranger?

Intermediate Grades

As students mature, fiction becomes a good medium to develop this skill of asking seemingly irrelevant as they can be asked to predict what might lie ahead in the story, to consider what could go wrong and how the characters might be blind-sided. Asking such questions is a basic aspect of making prediction.

- What should Michelle be asking at this point?
- What do you think she should be thinking about but has not been?
- What surprises are lying in wait for her?
- What are her blind spots?
- If you were giving her advice, what would it be?
- What's the worst that could happen to her?
- How should she prepare for the unexpected?

Middle School

As students begin to wrestle with problem-solving and problem-based learning, the opportunities abound for asking apparently irrelevant questions, as the development of action plans requires that they look ahead and anticipate issues and problems that might limit success.

- If the Army Engineer Corps takes down a half dozen dams on the Snake River, what could go wrong?
- What risks and issues have we failed to consider when drawing up our plan of action?
- What did we forget?
- What is the worst that can happen?
- What unthinkable catastrophe or surprise should we be thinking about?

Irrelevant Questions

High School

High school students continue to practice this skill at increasingly challenging levels, whether they be anticipating the problems Hamlet will encounter or predicting the twists and turns Fate has in store for Captain Ahab. Human blindness becomes a familiar theme, whether it be caused by arrogance, ignorance, greed or misplaced passions. Students can identify historical examples by the dozens, whether it be Napoleon attacking Russia or Saddam attacking Kuwait. They come to understand that apparently irrelevant questions often prove crucially important.

- How will hubris prove to be Frank's undoing?
- How could he be so blind?
- How does anyone protect themselves from such blindness?
- How do we figure out what we don't know?
- What can we expected in the way of the unexpected?
- What unthinkable turn of events is likely to surprise us?

Chapter 13 - Inventive Questions

"What can I make of this?"

At the end of the day (or the project), we expect students to come up with something new, to prove they are thinkers, not just collectors.

A thinker will employ inventive questions to transform information into insight. He or she will turn findings and data inside out and upside down seeking new possibilities. Inventive questions shift the research process from collection to creation as a thinker works on developing something new. This is high powered synthesis, not simple smushing. Wrestling with a challenging issue, students use such questions to fashion answers, create fresh solutions or develop novel plans of some kind.

- How do I make sense of these bits, bytes and pieces?
- What does all this information really mean?
- How can I rearrange what I have gathered so that some picture or new insight emerges?
- What needs to be eliminated, reversed or modified in order to make better sense of my findings?
- What is still missing?
- Can any information be regrouped or combined in ways which

Inventive Questions

help meaning to emerge?
- Can I display this information or data in a way which will cast more light on my essential question?

Such questions allow us to rearrange and modify the ideas and the information we have picked up along the way until we can shout "Aha!" and celebrate the discovery of something new.

Inventive questions should be uppermost in the thinker's mind while exploring and discovering. Instead of mere gathering, the thinker is engaged in creating new understandings, trying to fashion a solution to a problem, come up with a new idea or make a smart choice.

Examples of Inventive Questions

Primary Grades

We ask our youngest students to figure things out, applying their inferential reasoning skills to interpret a painting, a photograph, a collection of numbers, a poem or a story. They must read between the lines, put clues together and puzzle their way to comprehension.

- What's the story here?
- What's going on?
- What can I make of this?

Inventive Questions

Intermediate Grades

The complexity of the challenge deepens and intensifies as students reach the end of elementary school and their capacity to wrestle with abstraction grows. They continue to make meaning out of scraps of data or material that hints rather than states directly.

- Who is the leader of this group?
- What did the painter want us to feel?
- Why did the photographer shoot the picture from this angle?
- What's happening with crime in this city?
- Which city has the best weather according to this table of data?

Middle School

At this age, the student becomes capable of managing clusters of facts and evidence that must be woven together to form conclusions and sustain major generalizations.

- What does this particular story of hostage taking tell me about the captain's character?
- How does this story fit with the other stories I have been reading about his treatment of native people's on his last voyage?
- Do I have enough evidence to make a value judgment about his behavior?
- How much can I trust the view of Cook that comes through various accounts by members of his crew?
- How much can I trust Cook's versions of these events?
- How can I blend the various accounts together into some meaningful pattern?

High School

The high school student engages in theory testing and theory building, extrapolating from human experience to identify trends, tendencies and patterns.

- What makes some people so self destructive?
- What does it take to become a national leader?

Inventive Questions

- Is it possible to reach a position of power without losing one's idealism?
- Can a nation exploit its natural resources in a sustainable fashion?

Chapter 14 - Hypothetical Questions

Hypothetical questions are designed to explore possibilities and test relationships. They help us look into the future, wondering what might happen if certain conditions combine in various ways. They allow us to speculate, predict and wonder. We can project a theory or an option into a new setting or context. In theory, they make it possible to shake things up a bit.

- Suppose we took down all the dams on the Snake River.
- Suppose we privatized education.
- Suppose we transformed Social Security to allow private accounts and investments.
- Suppose we changed the definition of torture.
- What would happen if we offered big bounties on terrorists?
- How big a deficit can we run?
- What will happen when the deficit doubles?

Hypothetical questions are especially helpful when trying to decide between a number of choices or when trying to solve a problem. They are especially useful when we want to see if our hunches, our suppositions and our theories have any merit.

Examples of Hypothetical Questions

Primary Grades

In the primary grades we emphasize prediction. We ask students to look ahead when building things, when planning things and when reading stories. We help them to sharpen their understanding of cause and effect. We ask them to look before they leap. We argue the benefits of considering many options before making a decision. By asking what might happen if they select a particular option, they learn to compare and contrast choices rather than jumping to the first option that comes to mind.

- What will happen if I keep building this block tower higher?
- What kinds of supports will allow me to build higher without the

tower falling down?
- How did they build the cathedral so tall without the towers falling down?
- If I had a friend like Toad (In the "Frog and Toad" series) and he was throwing a tantrum over his lost button, what choices would I have to handle his tantrums?
- If I were the main character in this book we are reading, what could I do differently to avoid the troubles he keeps encountering?

Intermediate Grades

Science projects offer a rich opportunity to practice hypothetical questions since they are often designed to test one or more hypotheses. Classic projects of the past have included such studies as plant growth, exploring the consequences of restricting various key elements such as light, water or fertilizers. Social studies also offers many chances to consider options and their consequences, whether the students are studying explorers, native peoples or current events.

- What will happen to plant growth if I limit the amount of water for some of these plants and drown others?
- What would be a smart combination of light, water and fertilizer to promote growth?
- If Captain Cook had taken a stronger stand against those people who stole from him or hurt his crew, would they have behaved better and respected him more, or would they have protested, fought back and made life even worse for him?
- If the native people he encountered had been less receptive to his first visits and treated Cook and his men as invaders from the very beginning, would they have been better off?
- What might happen if we allow drilling for oil in Alaska?
- Are some types of drilling and exploration less damaging than others?
- What might happen if we do not allow drilling?
- Could another Tsunami happen in our life time? Are we better prepared for the next one? What can we do to prepare?

Middle School

Continuing with science projects and problem-based learning, we keep challenging students as they enter middle school to plan, predict

116

Hypothetical Questions

and hypothesize. While many of these activities may be based on role-playing, simulation and hypothetical situations, they provide safe practice for skills that will prove critically important to them as young adults.

- If I were appointed to a special commission in the Northern Territories assigned to create a plan to reduce gas sniffing among young ones, what strategies would have the best chance of working?
- If I were appointed to a planning group in my state charged with reducing the drop out rate, what strategies would have the best chance of working?
- If I were appointed to a planning group called together by the music industry to reduce the incidence of piracy, what strategies would have the best chance of working?
- If I were the main character in this story, what could I do differently to stay out of trouble?

High School

High school students develop increasingly powerful theory building and testing skills. We encourage them to apply these skills to larger projects extending over longer periods of time. As they near higher ed and actual work experiences we hope to equip them with the ability to plan strategically and thoughtfully.

- If this were my store, how could I turn around the sales trends?
- If I were operating this trucking business, what strategies would be most likely to optimize profits?
- If I were editor of this newspaper, how could I shift coverage of current events to attract a larger readership?
- If I were running the EPA, how could I have the best impact on the environment?
- If I were President, how would my foreign policy differ from the current policy?
- If I were writing this novel or short story, how would I improve it?

Chapter 15 - Probing Questions

Probing questions take us below the surface to the heart of the matter. They operate somewhat like the archeologist's tools - the brushes that clear away the surface dust and the knives that cut through the accumulated grime and debris to reveal the outlines and ridges of some treasure. Another appropriate metaphor might be exploratory surgery. The good doctor spends little time on the surface, knowing full well that the vital organs reside at a deeper level.

We learn to dig beyond the veneer. We are rarely satisfied with appearances. We expect our students to learn the same persistence and dogged determination.

> Every question we answer leads on to another question. This has become the greatest survival trick of our species.
> Desmond Morris

Some of the most skillful use of probing questions is displayed by reporters interviewing celebrities and leaders. While they may be seated in easy chairs and a comfortable setting like one's own living room, the atmosphere of such interviews is often highly charged with tension as the interviewer and interviewee play a game of cat and mouse.

The celebrity or leader usually wants to put a good spin on events, wants to project an attractive and wholesome persona, while the reporter plans to probe past these surface realities to reveal some deeper, more telling (or scandalous) truth. They both smile like old friends but maneuver like matador and bull.

Over the decades, probing questions have been associated with muckraking and exposés, scandals and corruption. When reporters stop asking such questions, we might worry about the health of the society since truth is often quite different from the PR versions of reality projected by government figures and leaders.

In a related trend, the society is fond of turning celebrities and historical figures into icons. Our students often read versions of these characters' lives that have been disneyfied - altered to make them more

Probing Questions

entertaining or suitable for family consumption. For them to gain a more realistic view, they must employ probing questions to scratch the surface glimmer and find out who they really were.

Detectives, reporters and scientists employ probing questions to grasp something substantial. It is a matter of digging. Sometimes this digging leads to dirt. Sometimes it uncovers truth.

Students can also develop digging skills that will serve them well, whether it be digging to understand a new employer, a new job, a new school or a new opportunity.

The ability to ask probing questions is a life skill that may partially protect one from spin, marketing and propaganda. Unfortunately, there is entirely too much distortion, pretense and dissembling. Probing questions offer a form of spin control and give truth in advertising an afterlife. Reality, sadly, is no longer what it used to be. Probing questions allow us to get reacquainted.

Examples of Probing Questions

Primary Grades

Very young children enjoy listening to detective stories as well as the chance to play detective. They welcome opportunities to search for clues and solve mysteries. In addition, they spend lots of time digging in sand, dirt, and mud. They may try to dig to China or dig for diamonds and other treasures. The primary teacher may harness this natural inclination to give students opportunities to practice probing questions.

Probing Questions

- In this story, the magician is trying to sell the boy magic beans, but what questions should the boy ask before buying what he is selling?
- What questions should we ask about this box of cereal to find out if it is healthy for us to eat?
- If we were trying to decide whether to play a sport or join a team, what questions should we ask?
- If you were the detective in this story and you heard the old man tell his story, what questions would you want to ask him?
- If a famous person from history came to visit our class, what questions would you ask to figure out what kind of person she/he was?
- If the Selfish Giant were here in person, what questions would you want to ask him to understand why he closed his garden to the children?

Intermediate Grades

As students grow in maturity and skill, the detective theme continues and extends to more types of mysteries, whether they be mysteries of human behavior or mysteries of the planet and natural world. The students sharpen their ability to ask probing questions that support inference, interpretation and understanding. They gain in ability to read between the lines and figure things out.

- In this painting of two older people called "Mates" what is the relationship between the man and the woman?
- Why is the man seated so far behind her?
- Why is he dressed up with jacket and tie?
- What can we learn from their facial expressions?
- What can we learn from her clenched hands?
- How can we predict when volcanoes will erupt or Tsunamis will strike?
- Are there warning signs?
- Do we have an adequate warning system here?
- If we had a visit from the agency responsible for setting up warning systems, what questions should we ask to see if we are safe?

Middle School

With an increasing focus on problem-based learning at this level,

121

Probing Questions

students will need skill with probing questions to identify the underlying factors contributing to the problem at hand. In order to deal with root causes rather than surface symptoms, questions drive a diagnostic process intended to identify the most promising opportunities for intervention.

Students at this level continue to sharpen their interviewing skills and their investigation competencies. They learn to focus their questioning where it will pay the best dividends, shifting attention strategically from topic to topic much like a prospector. Prospectors look for the presence of several promising geological factors in a location before drilling or digging. They know that this convergence of factors signals increased prospects for gold, oil or whatever treasure they seek.

Investigations work in a similar fashion, as the researcher cannot turn over every stone but must combine logic and intuition to delve into those sources that offer the best returns for the time spent.

Middle school students can begin to learn this process during simulated decision-making activities and research projects that call for inventive problem-solving.

- If twelve guests were present on the evening of Aunt Gertrude's murder, which ones might deserve the least questioning and which three would I question most extensively based on the brief sketches I have read about all twelve?
- If the two local candidates for Town Council visit and invite questions, what local issue will give me the best sense of their beliefs and politics? How can I frame a question that will require them to be specific and clear?
- How can I make effective use of follow-up questions to probe past the first sound bite answers?
- Are we now safe from the kind of huge power failure that hit the East coast of the USA a few years ago? How can I find out? What questions should I ask to test the quality of current plans and strategies? How will I know if I am just getting PR instead of substance? Who on this list of dozens of experts, commentators, critics, journalists, lobbyists, interest groups and officials should I contact to double check these claims?
- Is the current government strategy to protect the Victorian coast adequate? How can I find out? What questions should I ask to test the quality of current plans and strategies? How will I know if I am just getting PR instead of substance? Who should I contact to double check these claims?

High School

Probing Questions

As with all of the questioning types, we expect to see high school students employing probing questions to explore increasingly complex scenarios, problems and issues. Preferably, those scenarios and issues will pass tests of authenticity and credibility, resonating with students' view of the so-called real world. Hopefully, students will practice this kind of questioning beyond school, learning to ask good questions during work and community experiences.

- If I am interviewing for a job and the boss asks me if I have any questions to ask, what questions will reflect well on me but also help me decide if it is a healthy organization and a good place to work?
- If I were hired to come up with a new plan for a town strategy on homelessness, who would I interview and what questions would I ask them to gain an understanding of the problem and the best solutions?
- NASA has suffered from several disasters that some commentators claim could have been avoided if it were not for some organizational weaknesses. What would be the best way to assess the veracity of this claim? Who would I interview? What questions would I ask?
- A number of nations have awkward, painful and sometimes disgraceful histories when it comes to the treatment of native populations by newcomers. Does the concept of reconciliation have value? Has anyone done it well? How would I find out? Who should I ask? What should I ask them?

Chapter 16 - Divergent Questions

Divergent questions intentionally explore unfamiliar terrain with the expectation that new ideas and possibilities frequently emerge from such unexplored regions.

Unlike irrelevant questions, divergent questions use existing knowledge as a base from which to kick off like a swimmer making a turn. They move more logically from the core of conventional knowledge and experience.

Divergent questions are more carefully planned to explore territory adjacent to that which is known or understood. The researcher gradually extends coverage but avoids the kinds of leaps typical of irrelevant questions.

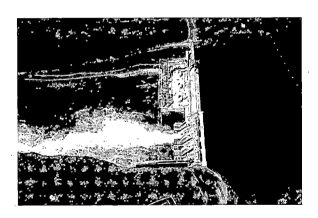

Trying to find a way to restore salmon stocks in the Pacific Northwest?

- Has anyone ever been successful in this region?
- What did they try?
- Was anyone successful elsewhere in places like the New England or Scotland?
- What did they try?

Divergent Questions

- Has anyone been successful with other types of fish?
- What did they try?
- Has anyone been successful with other species?
- What did they try?
- Are there some approaches to salmon restoration worth discarding?
- Are there some basic traps to avoid when trying to save any species?

If we limit our search to successful attempts, we may miss out on the chance to avoid other people's mistakes. Sometimes we learn more by studying the opposite of our main target.

In the same sense, we may want to check out efforts to restore air quality and other tangentially related efforts. We may even explore efforts to reintroduce endangered species to various habitats.

New ideas are rarely sitting waiting for us in obvious places. The ability to freely associate related topics and questions greatly increases the odds that researchers will make important discoveries.

Examples of Divergent Questions

Primary Grades

With very young children we hope to alert them to rich sources lying outside the lines, encouraging them to question, color and think past the boundaries of obvious thought. We nurture a spirit of exploration and welcome the flights of a vivid imagination. This is not always easy in schools because so much attention in the early years is devoted to showing students how to produce correct answers. Convergence, correctness and conventionality are often prized above divergence and imagination. Color inside the lines! Follow the rules! Do as I say!

Teachers must seek a healthy balance between order, logic, chaos and inspiration, helping students to value the mix and avoid the extreme.

- What questions should the girl in this story ask to make sure she is prepared for the trip ahead? Is there anything she has forgotten? Is there anything she may have left behind that she will need? How could other travellers help her know what questions to ask?
- The king in this story seems blind in some respects. What ques-

126

Divergent Questions

tions should he ask that he has not asked? What will happen to him because he did not ask?

- Are there questions I should be asking about my own life but forgot to ask?
- If I were asked to invent a new toy, what questions should I ask?
- If I have a new brother or sister coming into my home, what questions should I ask? How can I be a great brother or sister?
- If I plan to write a poem that is rich in terms of the words I use, how can I ask questions about the five senses that will help me?
- How did this painter make something beautiful by breaking the rules?

Intermediate Grades

During the upper elementary grades, students can employ cluster diagrams and mind maps to map out promising territory for exploration, as one list might show what they know and another might identify what they do not know or understand.

- If I were planning a new town for several thousand people what questions should I ask of them before I plan the town? What questions should I ask of other planners who have tried to build such towns? What questions should I ask of the people who have lived in their new towns?
- The main character in this story seems to ignore some very important issues and questions. If I were him, what questions would I want to explore before making a final decision or plan?
- If I wanted to improve my essay, what questions should I be asking? How might the Six Traits approach help me form good questions?
- The European explorers often failed to consider issues and questions we consider important today. What questions should they have considered with regard to native people, for example?
- If I were hired on a team to fix the traffic problems of this town, what questions should I explore to make sure I give the challenge a complete look?
- Now that I have mapped out what I know about the issue or problem I am studying, what seems to be missing? Are there major categories of questions that I have neglected to list or consider?

Divergent Questions

Middle School

As students continue with science projects and problem-based learning entering middle school, we keep challenging them to extend their research and the discovery process into territory that, while unfamiliar, is logically related to what they would normally consider. They expand their ability to notice or uncover these related regions.

- If I am trying to improve on a disaster plan for earthquakes for our town, what can I learn by looking at plans for other kinds of natural disasters such as floods, storms and volcanic eruptions?
- What can I learn by looking at plans for other kinds of disasters such as chemical spills, nuclear power plant leaks or terrorist attacks?
- What can I learn by considering plans for less serious but still challenging situations like the leaving of a major sporting stadium after a contest?
- What can I learn by looking at plans for normal traffic flow and transportation systems?
- What can I learn by considering all of these questions in terms of other towns, states, regions and countries?
- What can I learn to add to my list by interviewing experts in such planning?
- What can I learn to add to my list by interviewing victims of such disasters?
- What can I learn to add to my list by interviewing relief agencies?

High School

As high school students apply questioning skills to larger projects extending over longer periods of time, we expect to see the mapping mentioned earlier grow increasingly sophisticated, as students learn to move in several different directions when extending the reach of their research, sliding their minds across the landscape of their issues almost like crabs sliding sideways.

In the middle school example above, the student moved first from one type of natural disaster to other types. Then the student moved to types of disasters not caused naturally. Next we saw a shift to less serious situations, and after that the student considered operating procedures. To avoid a local or provincial point of view, the student added a series of geographical moves. Finally, hoping to identify even

Divergent Questions

more questions, the student requests assistance from a range of groups. High school students would use similar strategies at deeper levels of complexity.

- In preparing for this debate on foreign policy, how can I anticipate the arguments the other team will make, map them and then use them to point me toward counter arguments, issues and questions that I might not have considered if I only concentrated on building a case for our own team's position?
- When trying to figure out if Hemingway's description was really so powerful, what other writers are renowned for their description and what questions should I ask about their writing that would help me judge his?
- How can I map out what I know about acid rain to show what I don't know but need to know?

Chapter 17 - Provocative Questions

Provocative questions are meant to push against tradition, to challenge routines and to stimulate fresh thinking, throwing conventional wisdom off balance and dogma into a defensive posture.

Such questions may give free rein to doubt, disbelief and skepticism. They often kick up dust, create dissonance and inspire reappraisal and reconsideration.

> The best servants of the people, like the best valets, must whisper unpleasant truths in the master's ear. It is the court fool, not the foolish courtier, whom the king can least afford to lose.
>
> Walter Lippmann

Ancient empires and kingdoms in China often employed a court jester or fool whose job it was to challenge and make fun of policies and ideas and key players surrounding the king or queen. The fool could often get away with a level of questioning that would never have been permitted a "legitimate" member of the council.

On the other hand, the fool might also lose his head if the king or queen took offense. A dangerous occupation!

Closely associated with divergent questions and irreverent questions, provocative questions help provide the basis for satire, parody, and exposés whether they be **Gulliver's Travels, Alice in Wonderland,** or a cartoon strip like **Dilbert.**

These plays and stories poke fun at politicians and leaders in ways that help protect us from excessive deference or what is sometimes called "spin" today.

Schools may have devoted too little attention to showing students how to make use of irony, satire and parody, yet these art forms are sorely needed to keep our systems and institutions open and vibrant.

When inspired by a desire for the truth, provocative questions may help to debunk propaganda, mythologies, hype, bandwagons and big lies. They can scrape away layers of bunk, dismiss blather and determine if there is substance worth considering. In a time of what Toffler

Provocative Questions

calls "info-tactics" such questions are an essential tool.
   In an age of info-glut and info-garbage, we must equip students to
pose questions that enable them to sort out meaning and identify value.

- Where's the beef? the content? the substance? the logic? the
   evidence?
- What is the source? Is the source reliable?
- What's the point? Is there a point?
- Cutting past the noise and the rhetoric, is there any insight,
   knowledge or worthwhile information here?

Examples of Provocative Questions

Primary Grades

   This question type is not a priority with the youngest students, but
we can work to build some healthy skepticism at this age, using advertising, product boxes and Web pages as a source. While being careful
not to overemphasize the negative, we do want to alert them to the
many cultural messages aimed at their age group by marketers and
others whether it be during Saturday morning TV programs or walking
through the grocery store with their parents.

- How much sugar do they put in this cereal?
- Why do so many toys seem less fun than the ad once you buy
   them and bring them home?
- What tricks do advertisers use in ads for kids?

Intermediate Grades

   At this age, students can develop critical thinking abilities that
allow them to cut past exaggerated claims, false promises and appeals
to fad, fears and fashion, yet they are also entering a stage during
which they take some comfort in figuring out what it means to be cool,
what shoes one must wear to school and how to blend in or stand out.
   We continue to use advertising and Web sites as source material to
develop their critical thinking skills, but we also take advantage of
history to show them propaganda and government abuses of the past.

- How did the artist who made this poster try to convince me the
   Huns were terrible?
- During the early years of our country, the Mother Country

132

sometimes treated us unfairly, but those who complained and urged rebellion were called traitors to the King. Today we call many of them patriots. How can someone be called a traitor and patriot all at the same time?
• Which of these six cereal boxes uses the worst tricks in reporting its nutritional content?
• How did the creators of this Web site distort truth and try to manipulate the facts to convince visitors of a particular point of view?

Middle School

As students come to middle school, we begin asking that they assume the role of historical figures in simulations and we engage them in problem-solving exercises which require careful thought about complex issues and the influence of organizations on possible solutions. Their capacity to understand the dynamics of organizations grows as they see that issues are rarely a matter of black and white, right and wrong.

• If I had been a member of the team developing nuclear weapons for the Americans during World War II, what ethical questions should I have been considering?
• If I had been FDR or Truman at that time, what ethical questions should I have been considering?
• If I had been a member of U.S. or Australian military at the time, what strategic questions should I have been considering?
• If I had been a member Japanese military at the time, what strategic questions should I have been considering?
• What questions should the father have considered in the novel, **The Yearling**? What questions would I have asked if I had been the son?

High School

The process deepens as students reach high school. They read more stories of complex issues, see movies depicting moral dilemmas and consider historical and current events tinged with many shades of gray.

• How did Howard Hughes as depicted in the movie, **The Aviator**, employ provocative questions as he tried to change the movie

Provocative Questions

industry and the aviation industry?
- What important questions did Macbeth forget to ask as he rose to power in Scotland?
- Did Hamlet do a good job with provocative questions?
- What provocative questions should scientists be asking these days?
- What provocative questions should corporate boards be asking these days?
- What provocative questions should movie producers and TV producers be asking these days?
- What provocative questions should news editors be asking these days?

Chapter 18 - Unanswerable Questions

It may seem strange that unanswerable questions deserve mention at all. If they are unanswerable, one might argue against their inclusion on any list of question types, but they rank highly in terms of import. Because they explore profound and often baffling territory, they may defy solution and leave us feeling incomplete. They are bristling with perplexities.

Unanswerable questions can be approached. They can be considered and pondered. One can even build tentative, partial answers to such questions. But they stubbornly elude final, conclusive or satisfying answers.

- How will I or should I be remembered?
- How much can anyone resist Fate's will?
- What is the good life?
- What is friendship?
- How would life be different if . . .

Such questions are pivotal, central and defining.

When exploring such questions, we must usually be content with "casting light" upon them.

When wrestling with unanswerable questions, we may never capture some exact and completely satisfying truth, but we can extend our level of understanding and reduce the opacity of the darkness.

The real questions are the ones that obtrude upon your consciousness whether you like it or not, the ones that make your mind start vibrating like a jackhammer, the ones that you "come to terms with" only to discover that they are still there.

The real questions refuse to be placated. They barge into your life at the times when it seems most important for them to stay away. They are the questions asked most frequently and

Unanswerable Questions

answered most inadequately, the ones that reveal their true
natures slowly, reluctantly, most often against your will.
Ingrid Bengis

Ironically, the more important the issue or the challenge, the greater the likelihood that it will be somewhat unanswerable. Paradox, ambiguity and resistance to capture are typical traits of such questions. We cannot seem to "get our heads around them." Try as we may, it is difficult to get a grip.

- Will I be safe if I move to this new city or country?
- Will I be happier if I pick the path less traveled?
- What does this poem mean?
- Will the next decade be better than the last?
- What happened to the media?
- What happened to trust?
- How can we restore trust once it is lost?

Some organizational trainers proclaim the need for *tolerance of ambiguity*, but ***management of ambiguity*** seems like a more powerful notion, as the first phrase hints at passivity and acceptance while the second requires action and engagement.

We expect our students to grapple with the important but obscure and cloudy issues, not back away from them. At the same time, we need to prepare them for uncertainty and incompletion so they will value the partial answer and shrug off the desire for certainty.

It is a matter of viewing life from many perspectives as well as many shades of gray rather two tone black and white.

Even the youngest children need to understand that some questions are difficult to answer without discouraging them, overburdening them or souring them to the search for understanding. As early as the age of four, children ask many questions that adults have difficulty answering.

- Why does rain fall down?
- How big is the sky?
- Why do we have war?
- Why do some parents hurt their children?

Because even these very young children are bombarded on a daily basis by media messages rich in violence, scandal and disaster, they cannot help but ask why. They cannot help but ask for reassurance.

Unanswerable Questions

We can and should try to shelter the very young from this bombardment knowing that a continuing exposure to horrific events is not healthy, but we must also acknowledge that such sheltering cannot be completely successful in a society that wraps us all in such images wherever we go, with large flashing screens glowing down at us from the sides of buildings and advertising aimed at us from every corner and every angle.

The young must learn to cope with the bombardment, filtering, blocking, ignoring and deflecting those messages and that content that do not belong, but this kind of protective deflection requires a high level of self awareness and reflection. Surrounded by violent toys and games, the young can easily immerse themselves in virtual worlds that mirror the worst of the headlines and the daily news.

Examples of Unanswerable Questions

Primary Grades

Students come to school asking lots of unanswerable questions, so it is largely a matter of encouraging the continuance of such questioning by employing techniques like Debbie Miller's "Wonder Boxes" - a strategy that calls for first graders to fill refrigerator boxes with questions as they arise. Some of these will call for factual answers, but many will be unanswerable.

• What is a good friend?
• How can a good friend hurt you?
• How can some parents hurt or neglect their own children?
• Why do we have war?
• What is the best way to show love?
• Why did the character in this story act so selfishly?
• What made Sam into a bully?
• How can we make sure there are no bullies?

Unanswerable Questions

Intermediate Grades

If we do a good job of keeping their sense of wonder alive during the first years of schooling, student questioning behaviors should thrive into the upper elementary grades, but many teachers reading this book may encounter students at this age whose questioning propensities have been blunted and discouraged in previous years. They may have to restore and reawaken them, reminding students how to explore issues and questions that are important or intriguing.

- What will the future bring?
- Why is there so much bad news?
- What should I do with my life?
- What should I do about my brother? sister? parents?
- How can I become a champion?
- What makes some people trustworthy and others untrustworthy?
- Why did some explorers act nobly part of the time and horribly at other times?

Middle School

Middle school students find much of life baffling and questionable. Emerging from the trusting certainties of pre-adolescence, they suddenly begin to wonder if the adults know much of anything about anything. It seems to many adolescents that adults have made quite a mess of many things and there is a general tendency to question the wisdom, fairness and sense of many rules, restrictions and procedures. This inclination to doubt and question can be harnessed to promote smart thinking instead of tiresome whining and complaining, but the challenge is not a simple one.

- What is the best way to make friends in middle school?
- How can I make the team?
- How can I get my parents to trust me?
- Why don't we take better care of the environment?
- Should I join the military when I am older?
- How will I ever afford to go to college? Should I go?
- What should I do with my life?
- How can I be proud of myself?
- How can I make my parents proud of me?
- How can I learn to write like the authors we have been reading?
- Should I become a scientist? Would I be happy?
- How important is money when picking a career?

Unanswerable Questions

- What is a good citizen? a good leader? a good governor? a good president?
- Are some wars good wars?

High School

By the time they reach high school, many students have figured out that many of the most important questions are unanswerable at some level, but they grow increasingly accepting of these limitations and ambiguities, grasping that adults must grapple with complications children could not imagine. Their new found pragmatism is sometimes worn proudly as a kind of sophistication. Some embrace the gray and imprecise qualities of life as a sign that they are becoming worldy wise.

- Was Gatsby worldly wise?
- Would Donald Trump or Martha Stewart make good bosses?
- How can I maintain my ideals when there is so much wrong with the world and so many greedy, evil people?
- Which of the characters and leaders we have studied this year are worth emulating?
- Is it worth joining a political party, registering and voting?
- How do people in other countries view us?
- Is there such a thing as good science?
- Is it possible to have a career in business and still maintain ethics?
- Where am I headed?

Chapter 19 - Subsidiary Questions

Telling - Organizing - Clarifying - Organzing Sorting & Sifting, Elaborating, Planning and Strategic Questions

This group of question types comes into play early in the investigation as the thinker begins mapping the territory needing exploration. They work in concert.

Subsidiary Questions

In some respects, subsidiary questions do not deserve a "type" of their own, since all questions other than essential questions start as subsidiary questions but then move after birth to some other question type once their function is clear.

These are questions that combine to help us build answers to our essential questions. Essential questions spawn families of related questions that lead to insight. The more skillful our students become at formulating and then categorizing subsidiary questions, the more success they will have constructing new knowledge. All of the question categories listed in the *Toolkit* other than essential questions are subsidiary questions.

Students have several strategies from which to choose when generating a comprehensive list of subsidiary questions for an investigation:

• They can brainstorm and list every question that comes to mind, utilizing a huge sheet of paper, a word processing program or a graphical organizing program such as Inspiration™ capturing questions as they come to mind. Later they should move questions around until they end up grouped along side of related questions.

• Students can also employ a list of question types like the ones outlined in this book to generate questions. This approach helps provoke thought and questions in categories they might not otherwise consider.

Subsidiary Questions

Telling Questions

Telling questions lead us like a so-called smart bomb right to the target. They are built with such precision that they provide sorting and sifting during the gathering or discovery process. They focus the investigation so that we gather only the very specific evidence and information we require, only those facts which "cast light upon" or illuminate the main question at hand

The better the list of telling questions generated by the researcher, the more efficient and pointed the subsequent searching and gathering process. A search strategy may be profoundly shifted by the development of telling questions.

If a student is trying to pick a city with good weather, rather than collect every thing available on climate and weather for a dozen cities, she or he decides what three factors mean the most. If sunny days, lack or rain and reasonably warm temps are the critical issue, then the telling question captures those three factors and places the focus of the research right where it belongs.

"Which of these twelve cities offers the best combination of sunny days, little rain and reasonably warm temperatures?"

Because telling questions make it possible for students to cut to the chase, eliminating wasted time and irrelevant information, teachers must provide practice in several aspects of writing such questions. First of all, teachers must help students understand the concept of prime factors or priorities, since deciding upon priorities is basic to the process of narrowing focus. Once the priorities are clarified, the teacher shows how to translate those priorities into specific data collecting questions.

"What is the average annual rainfall in Beijing?"

Telling questions can prove very efficient, but their effectiveness is directly related to the precision with which the student defines the terms. Much like good kitchen knives, telling questions can only do their job if kept quite sharp.

Organizing Questions

Organizing questions make it possible to structure findings into

Subsidiary Questions

categories that will allow students to construct meaning. Without these structures we suffer from hodge podge and mish mash - information collections akin to trash heaps and landfills, large in mass, lacking in meaning. The less structure we create in the beginning, the harder it becomes later to find patterns and relationships in the fragments or the collection of bits and pieces. Coherence is directly related to insight.

In making a choice of cities or a choice of ship captains, for example, the student must decide upon criteria. The question leading to criteria is an example of an organizing question.

"What are the traits of a great ship captain?"

This question will establish the organizing categories for data collection:

• Navigation skill?
• Good listener?
• Courageous?
• Resourceful?
• Inspiring?
• Clever?
• Honest?
• Fair?
• Commanding?

Each time students come upon valuable findings, they extract the relevant data and place them where they belong.
For a choice of cities, they might develop the following criteria:

• Malls
• Art Museums
• Pizza
• Sports
• Climate
• Crime
• Job
• Tolerance
• Diversity
• Liberty
• Opportunity
• Justice
• Health

Subsidiary Questions

Once they have found data on average annual rainfall, they place them where they belong.

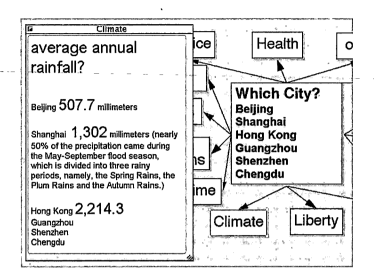

In the diagram above, a note is attached to the Climate cluster into which will go all the pertinent data.

Our challenge is teaching students to paraphrase, condense and then place their findings thoughtfully rather than cutting and pasting huge blocks of text which have been unread, undigested and undistilled. We teach them to collect "just the right stuff." Pertinence takes on major significance as a value to guide research and collection.

Clarification Questions

Clarification questions help convert fog and smog into meaning. A collection of facts and opinions does not always make sense by itself.

Hits do not equal TRUTH. A mountain of information may do more to block understanding than promote it.

Defining words and concepts is central to this clarification process. Finding the correct technical terms can lead to much more valuable findings than one might uncover using casual or informal language.

For this reason, we encourage students to spend some time doing background reading that will help them to identify key concepts and

Subsidiary Questions

phrases that will prove useful. This will help them in the search process, but clarification questions are also important as part of the interpretation process. Once we have gathered information, what does it mean? Can we trust it? Can we make sense of it?

- What do they mean by "violent crime rate?" Do they use the same definition and standards as the FBI?
- What do they mean by "declining rate of increase?"
- How did they gather their data? Was it a reliable and valid process? Do they show the data and evidence they claim to have in support of their conclusions? Was is substantial enough to justify their conclusions?
- Did they gather evidence and data?

Examining the coherence and logic of an argument, an article, an essay, an editorial or a presentation is crucial.

- How did they develop the case they are presenting?
- What is the sequence of ideas and how do they relate one to another?
- Do the ideas logically follow one from the other?

Determining the underlying assumptions is vital.

- How did they get to this point?
- Are there any questionable assumptions below the surface or at the foundation of the argument?

Sorting & Sifting Questions

Sorting and sifting questions enable us to manage info-glut and info-garbage - the hundreds of pages and files which often rise to the surface when we conduct a search - culling and keeping only the information which is pertinent and useful. Relevancy is the prime criterion employed to determine which pieces of information are saved and which are tossed overboard. We create a net of questions to allow all but the most important information to slide away. We then place the good information with the questions it illuminates.

- Which parts of this information are worth keeping?
- Where should I put those parts?
- Will this information shed light on any of my questions?"

Subsidiary Questions

- Is this information reliable?
- How much of this information do I need to place in my database or cluster diagram?
- How can I summarize the best information and ideas?
- Are there any especially good quotations?
- What information should I retain for citation purposes?

Elaborating Questions

Elaborating questions extend and stretch the import of what we are finding. They take the explicit and see where it might lead. They also help us to plum below surface to implicit meanings.

- What does this mean?
- What might it mean if certain conditions and circumstances changed?
- How could I take this farther? What is the logical next step? What is missing? What needs to be filled in?
- Reading between the lines, what does this REALLY mean?
- What are the implied or suggested meanings?

Planning Questions

Planning questions lift us above the action of the moment and require that we think about how we will structure our search, where we will look and what resources we might use such as time and information. If we were sailing west on a square masted ship, we would pass off the wheel and the lines to teammates in order to climb to the crow's nest - a lofty perch from which we could look over the horizon.

Too many researchers, be they student or adult, make the mistake of burying their noses in their studies and their sources. They have trouble seeing the forest, so close do they stand to the pine needles. They are easily lost in a thicket of possibilities.

The effective researcher develops a plan of action in response to Ppanning questions like these:

Sources

- Who has done the best work on this subject?
- Which group may have gathered the best information?
- Which medium (Internet, CD-ROM, electronic periodical collection, scholarly book, etc.) is likely to provide the

Subsidiary Questions

most reliable and relevant information with optimal efficiency?
• Which search tool or index will speed the discovery process?

Sequence

What are all of the tasks which need completing in order to generate a credible product which offers fresh thought backed by solid evidence and sound thinking?

Strategic Questions

Strategic questions focus on ways to make meaning. The researcher must switch from tool to tool and strategy to strategy while passing through unfamiliar territory. Closely associated with the planning questions formulated early on in this process, strategic questions arise during the actual hunting, gathering, inferring, synthesizing and ongoing questioning process.

• What do I do next?
• How can I best approach this next step?, this next challenge? this next frustration?
• What thinking tool is most apt to help me here?
• What have I done when I've been here before? What worked or didn't work? What have others tried before me?
• What type of question would help me most with this task?
• How do I need to change my research plan?

Sometimes we ask students to pursue answers to questions that are not worthy of much effort or attention.
"How many gargoyles are there on the Cathedral of Notre Dame?"
Who really cares?

An eleventh grade student had sent me an e-mail message. "Can you help me?" Her teacher had a set of extra credit questions. Tough questions. But why would anyone need to know how many gargoyles perch upon the ramparts of the Cathedral of Notre Dame de Paris?

The question was my teachers idea. he always asks a bunch of extra credit questions....example, the little holes in your shoes that your shoe laces go through is what. that was one of our questions last week. it gives a fun swing to Advance Vocabulary. he gave us this one bout the gargoyles a month ago and he said that he had given that one for over 10 years and that no one in any of his classes has EVER found the answer. i am gonna take him some of these e-mails and show them to him tomorrow durin class. he says he will not get on the comp to look b/c he thinks that "the Computer is the portal to hell' pretty funny. well... maybe we can find it sooner or later.

From Trivial Pursuit

An exhaustive search led to little illumination , but the Office of Tourism made a valiant effort (e-mail below).

Hi and thanks for your informations !

We are still waiting and looking for new elements. We were also told by Mr. Fonquernie's assistant that the number of gargoyles is not same than when the Cathedral Notre-Dame was built : some broke, there were destructions, some gar goyles were added later ...

A certain number of gargoyles are not apparent (we do not yet know if they all will appear on the architect's plans) ...
We will be very pleased to be included in your article although we are sorry we could not help you more !
Your question definitely passioned us ;-)

Thanks and best regards
David
Office de Tourisme et des Congres de Paris
75008 Paris

There are so many more important and more intriguing questions we could explore about gargoyles. When we limit students to trivial pursuit, we make a mockery of authentic research and deprive them of a chance to explore the tough issues, choices, dilemmas and questions that really matter.

• Why did people place gargoyles on cathedrals?
• What good are gargoyles?

• How are gargoyles and chimeras different? Which are better?
• Why does this cat sit with the gargoyle?
• Why does the gargoyle sit with the cat?
• Why do some people place gargoyles on their desks?
• Why do some people place gargoyles in their gardens?
• Why do some people place gargoyles on their office buildings?

From Trivial Pursuit

- What kinds of people like gargoyles? Why?
- Are some gargoyles better than others?
- What are the traits or characteristics of a good gargoyles? Should they be fierce and threatening? Kind, gentle and welcoming?
- How should modern gargoyles be different from the ancient ones? Why?
- Which of the gargoyles below would make the best one for your house or garden? Why?

Gargoyle 1   Gargoyle 2   Gargoyle 3

- Do we still need gargoyles? Why?
- Will we always need gargoyles? Why?
- How do other cultures like Bali islanders and Hindus make use of figures carved in wood or stone?
- In what ways are such figures or gargoyles like icons?
- How do icons influence the quality of life and our culture? Are they healthy? Unhealthy?
- Why do some celebrities become icons? Are some celebrities like gargoyles?

Some call such questions essential questions because they call upon our best thinking and touch upon those matters that define what it means to be human. They are questions that help us to make meaning out of the events and circumstances of our lives.

There is a huge difference between knowledge on the one hand and understanding or insight on the other hand.

Schools often engage students in collecting answers, in accumulating information. But essential questions require that students spend time pondering the meaning and importance of information.

Essential questions are questions that resonate within our hearts and our souls. They are central to our lives. Most important thought during our lives will center on such essential questions.

From Trivial Pursuit

A central theme of this book has been the importance of moving past trivial pursuit to questions and matters of import.

Whether we ask students to study gargoyles, presidents, ship captains or cities, let's make sure they examine issues that pass the test of "So what?"

Chapter 21 - The Great Question Press

No more trivial pursuit.

No more topical research.

No more hunts for simple facts - deadly, tiresome and lacking in value, mind-numbing activities without import.

This chapter offers something like a cider press - but one that easily produces intriguing questions from the mass of curriculum content that usually inspires mere collection or varieties of trivial pursuit.

Try the **Question Press** on standard content and watch your students squeeze meaning out of inert matter.

Give them a lift. Engage them in making up their own minds. Equip them to manage the tough questions of life.

Questions of Import

Like essential questions, questions of import are worthy of our time but are also likely to spark interest and awaken curiosity. They require thought rather than mere collection of facts or simple cut-and-paste thinking.

Resonance — there is no wisdom without it. Resonance is a natural phenomenon, the shadow of import alongside the body of fact, and it cannot flourish except in deep time.

The Gutenberg Elegies by Sven Birkerts - Page 75

Dimensions of Questioning

Previous chapters stressed the importance of students learning how to wield different types of questions to figure out complex issues and problems.

Questions work together as a system. As we begin to orchestrate various question types in the pursuit of understanding, we expand our

The Great Question Press

capacity to think and act in smart ways. We gain in our ability to collect and fashion intelligence rooted in reality rather than presumption or wishful thinking. We are protected somewhat from bias, ideology and narrow thinking.

We learn to seek truth wherever it may be. Unlike these boys on an Australian beach digging to China, we do not always dig straight down. We do not fall into the trap of silo thinking.

After sustained practice with challenging questions, students become skillful at juggling combinations of questions to make sense of their world.

The Great Question Press

Use the chart below to fashion demanding questions from your curriculum content. Pick a function, read the sample questions and then start writing your own.

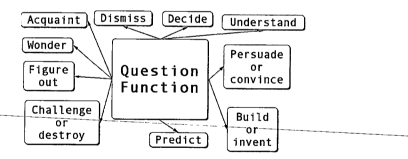

Understand ──────────────────────────

In popular terms, the goal of this questioning activity is to "get one's head around" some topic, idea, challenge or proposal. By the end, one hopes to grasp key traits, elements and structures.

Traditional Questions
1. Go find out about Robert or Elizabeth Browning (or any other

Transformed
1. What were the five most distinguishing characteristics of

The Great Question Press

poet, general, prime minister, hero, character, celebrity, scoundrel or seer. What did he or she do?

Browning and how did they contribute to her success of failure? What made her great or not so great? What are the two or three most important things you learned about her that might serve you well?

2. Go find out about the Victorian coast (or any other region, city, town, state, province or nation). How long is it? How many people live there? What is its climate?

2. What are the biggest challenges or threats facing the coast? Rank the ten biggest from highest to lowest import and explain why you rank them thus. What should be done about these challenges?

3. What are the chief points of interest in a city like Los Angeles?

3. Which museums, parks, entertainment facilities and points of interest listed by the encyclopedia for Los Angeles would actually be interesting and worth a visit? Which could you safely recommend to various people you know with different tastes and interests if you were planning a week long tour? Which are unworthy of a visit?

4. What are the main sections in Mozart's Piano Concerto?

4. When does this concerto begin to approach greatness? How does Mozart achieve these great moments musically? To what extent is it Mozart as composer as opposed to the pianist and performer's rendition that impress or move us? To what extent a blend?

Figure Out ───────────────────

This type of questioning unlocks an enigma, solves a mystery or completes a puzzle. While the process may commence with speculation, hypothesizing and supposing, the goal is to move toward understandings that are anchored in facts and reality.

The Great Question Press

Traditional	Transformed
1. Go find out about Richard Nixon (or Bill Clinton or any other important person).	1. Where did Nixon (or Clinton) go wrong? Why do you suppose he slipped from power and grace? What caused him the most trouble? What could you learn from his example?
2. Go find out about free trade. .	2. What are the hidden costs of free trade? What could we do to minimize risks and damage? How could we maximize benefits?
3. Find out about Osama Bin Laden.	3. Where could Bin Laden be hiding? Why is he so hard to capture? How does he think? How could we outfox him?
4. How does Social Security work?	4. How are we going to fund Social Security?

Decide

This questioning illuminates the key differences between several choices or will supply the basis for a judgment for a particular course of action.

Traditional	Transformed
1. Go find out what people have tried to do in order to prevent wars. .	1. Which approaches to preventing war have had the most success over the years? Why do you suppose this is so? Which have the best prospects for the current century?
2. Go find out about Robert Frost, Emily Dickinson and Adrienne Rich.	2. Which of these poets wrote the most illuminating and evocative works? What traits made their works superior? Which poets and poems may survive this century?
3. What do the candidates propose doing about Iraq?	3. Which candidate has the most credible and logical approach to bringing peace, stability and democracy to Iraq?

The Great Question Press

4. What is the
national budget
for education,
defense and
health?

4. What is the national budget for education,
defense and health? How would you shift our
spending priorities? Why?

Build or Invent ————————————————

This questioning supports construction or adaptation to meet special
conditions or requirements.

Traditional
1. Go find out
about acid rain (or
some other major
challenge facing
the nation).

Transformed
1. Imagine the governor of your state has asked
your team to come up with a plan to reduce the
damage being done by acid rain to state forests.
After reviewing what has been done in the past,
what would be the main thrust of your proposal
to restore healthy forests and moderate the im-
pacts of acid rain? How can you improve on past
efforts?

2. What did
General X do in
the Battle of Some
Big River?

2. Taking advantage of 20-20 hindsight, what do
you think General X should have done differently
during the Battle of Some Big River to reduce
casualties and block the enemy from winning the
war?

3. What is your
synopsis of the
novel **Dirt Music**
by Tim Winton?

3. Where did the story bog down, falter and
disappoint you? What could Winton have done
differently, do you suppose, to improve upon
those sections?

4. What can we
expect from
falling objects in
terms of velocity
and momentum?

4. How could you build a package to reduce the
chances of an egg breaking upon impact after
tumbling from the basket of a hot air balloon at
125 feet above the ground?

The Great Question Press

Persuade or Convince ─────────────

This questioning identifies the prime arguments on behalf of a proposal of some kind.

Traditional	Transformed
1. What did Marie Curie discover?	1. If you wanted to nominate Curie as the most influential scientist of her time, how would you support your case?
2. What are the main treatment choices for depression?	2. After exploring the treatment choices for your friend's depression, you grow concerned that he/she is being unduly swayed by a charming doctor who is urging a path that might do great damage. What evidence, logic and testimony can you offer that might help him/her achieve a more balanced and healthy perspective?
3. What are the campaign planks of the major parties?	3. Which party is most likely to address the major challenges of this town, city, state, province or nation in the most productive and constructive manner? What makes you think so? Why should I listen to you?
4. Which Australian novelists have achieved the most success with a global audience?	4. Which two or three Australian novelists should have achieved the most success with a global audience? Why them and not the others? Which ones have actually won the most acclaim? Does this seem fair? Why or why not?

Challenge or Destroy ─────────────

This questioning seeks out the chief weaknesses in an idea, an argument, a research project or a plan.

Traditional	Transformed
1. What were the events leading up to the beginning of	1. What were the chief weaknesses in the foreign policies of France, Britain and the United States vis a vis Germany and Japan

The Great Question Press

World War Two?

prior to World War Two? How could you have improved the policies?

2. What is the current space program for the USA?

2. Are we on the right track when it comes to funding NASA and the current space exploration program, or should we be making major changes or considering some of the ideas advanced by President Bush?

3. How was intelligence gathered and assessed prior to the recent attack on Iraq?

3. Do we need to modify the gathering and assessment of intelligence? If so, in what ways?

4. What happened to investments and pensions when the Dot Com bubble burst?

4. Why are people so easily seduced by speculative bubbles and what can we do to reduce their power to entrance and harm investors? How can we avoid endangering pensions in the future?

Acquaint

This questioning breeds familiarity and appreciation.

Traditional
1. What stories has Annie Proulx written?

Transformed
1. How have Annie Proulx's stories changed since she moved to Wyoming? Was this a good change? Where do you hope she might move next?

2. What does Sydney have to offer?

2. What are Sydney's chief charms? Which restaurants live up to or exceed their press? Which neighborhoods have the most soul? the most energy? the most quiet? the most crime and poverty?

3. Find out about Osama Bin Laden.

3. What are Bin Laden's chief weaknesses, his major vulnerabilities, his obsessions and the patterns most likely to lead to his downfall and capture?

159

The Great Question Press

| 4. Who are the candidates? | 4. What has this candidate done about the major issues of the day? Has he or she served me well? What are the chances he/she will serve me well in the future? |

Dismiss

This questioning dispatches that which is unworthy of consideration.

Traditional	**Transformed**
1. Go find out about Jack London, the author.	1. To what extent was Jack London a fraud? How did his public image, his fiction, his theories about the good life and his actual life conflict? Why did he die young?
2. What is our policy on jobs?	2. What is going wrong on the job front?
3. How does science explain the power of diseases like SARS to spread and kill?	3. To what extent is the power of SARS to spread and kill beyond the scope of science to explain?
4. What were George Bernard Shaw's main criticisms of his society?	4. When was Shaw off base and lacking in judgment?

Wonder

This type of questioning explores doubts or boundaries while entertaining unusual possibilities and marvels.

Traditional	**Transformed**
1. How did our nation's European explorers treat indigenous people they encountered?	1. What could we have done differently and how would that have changed the society that we are now?

160

The Great Question Press

2. What are we doing about Alzheimer's Disease?

2. What is the best we could do about Alzheimer's Disease? Are we caught up or blinded in some ways to potential solutions? Why does Alzheimer's Disease seem to be on the increase? Are we paying the price for some terrible environmental faux pas or for chemicals in our diet?

3. What is meant by "checks and balances?"

3. When have "checks and balances" failed to operate? How and why might such systems break down? How can we avoid disappointments?

4. What is the life of the artist? of the engineer? of the teacher? of the politician?

4. Could I find joy and well being as an artist? as an engineer? as a teacher? as a politician? How could I protect myself from the risks and make the most of such a life?

Predict ─────────────────────

This questioning hypothesizes about likely outcomes.

Traditional	Transformed
1. What are the cultural preferences of those living in nations such as Iran, Iraq, Syria and Saudi Arabia?	1. How does culture influence the development of democratic norms? What would it take to create a healthy and stable democratic government in nations such as Iran, Iraq, Syria and Saudi Arabia?
2. What went wrong during the Great Depression?	2. Could something like the Great Depression ever happen again?
3. Which scientific laws or principles have proven to be unreliable or inadequate as we	3. Which scientific laws currently held to be true are most likely to shift during the next decade? Which are least truth worthy? If we can't trust science, then how do we know what to do?

The Great Question Press

have extended and
deepened the range of
scientific understand-
ings?

4. What were the excesses of the previous decade?	4. When folks look back at these times in a decade, which excesses will they list?

Making Import Central

Arming the young with the skills to wrestle with the tough questions and conundrums of life should be a prime focus of schools and
teachers.

If you teach young ones to question and probe, you equip them to
do well on all kinds of tests - state tests, classroom tests and the tests
of life.

High scores on tests of comprehension and problem-solving can
only be achieved when students are urged to think, figure things out
and wrestle with tough questions.

The **Great Question Press** gives students the practice they need
to make sense of a confusing world and find meaning when nonsense
is the main song playing on the radio.

We must show students how to "Go Figure" - work through the
dilemmas, conundrums, paradoxes and challenges of life with skill,
perseverance and integrity, to wrestle with what Michael Leunig calls
"the difficult truth."

Chapter 22 - Assessing Growth in Questioning

Events in the past may be roughly divided into those which probably never happened and those which do not matter. This is what makes the trade of historian so attractive."

W. R. Inge (1860-1954)

How do we know if teachers and students are employing questions in more powerful ways? Unfortunately, some schools forget to design data collection to help steer a program forward. Gathering data provides a basis for adjusting, pruning, expanding and improving program strategies, while a lack of data can sustain denial, delusion and waste.

There are at least two strategies worth considering.

Informal Surveys

Schools can make use of informal surveys such as the two **QDP** (**Questioning Daily Practice**) surveys included in Appendix A and Appendix B of this book to measure student and teacher reports of questioning activities over time.

These two surveys were developed with an eye toward judging what Michael Fullan has called "daily practice." We hope to see what kinds of pedagogy teachers are employing and we hope to discover whether or not students are being challenged to employ powerful questioning strategies on a daily basis.

While developed for use with upper elementary school, middle school and high school students, the items may be adjusted by school teachers and schools for use with other age students. The surveys may not be republished by any other agencies or corporations without explicit permission from this author.

It is recommended that the **QDP** be done several times with both students and teachers during the first year of a program so as to track

Assessing Growth

growth over the course of time. In subsequent years, an annual assessment will probably suffice to provide a portrait of change.

Formal Instruments

Schools may employ more rigorous and formal instruments to measure the growth of actual student thinking skills and problem-solving abilities expected to improve as a result of sustained attention to questioning and wondering.

A list of such tests prepared by Robert H. Ennis (**An Annotated List of Critical thinking Tests**) can be found on line at this URL:

http://www.critical thinking.net/CTTestList1199.html

Ennis is the author of one test battery aimed at Grades 4-14 that the author of this book used productively while a superintendent in New Jersey, but there are several dozen on his list worth investigating and considering.

The Ennis test is the **Cornell Critical thinking Test, Level X** (1985), by Robert H. Ennis and Jason Millman. The Critical thinking Company at http://www.critical thinking.com (formerly Midwest Publications), PO Box 448, Pacific Grove, CA 93950. Multiple-choice, sections on induction, credibility, observation, deduction, and assumption identification.

References

Arnheim, Rudolf (1969) **Visual Thinking.** University of California Press.

Berliner, Paul f. **Thinking in Jazz.** (1994) University of Chicago Press.

Birkerts, Sven. (1994) **The Gutenberg Elegies : The Fate of Reading in an Electronic Age.** Faber and Faber.

Bloom, Benjamin. (1954). **Taxonomy of Educational Objectives. Handbook I: Cognitive Domain.** New York: Longmans, Green & Co.

Bruner, Jerome. (1990) **Acts of Meaning.** Cambridge: Harvard University Press.

Carson, Rachel. **The Sense of Wonder,** first published by Harper & Row in 1965.

Cushman, Kathleen. (1989) "Asking the essential questions: Curriculum Development," Old Horace (vol 5-17), , *Horace.* Vol. 5, #5. June 1989. http://www.essentialschools.org/cs/resources/view/ces_res/137

Deal, Terrence E. and Peterson, Kent D. (1998) **Shaping School Culture : The Heart of Leadership.** San Francisco: Jossey-Bass Publishers.

De Bino, Edward. "Lateral Thinking & Parallel Thinking." http://www.edwdebono.com/debono/lateral.htm

De Bino, Edward. (1985) **Six Thinking Hats.** Little Brown & Co.

Eberle, Bob. (1997) **SCAMPER.** Prufrock Press.

Ennis, Robert H. (1999) **An Annotated List of Critical Thinking Tests.** http://www.criticalthinking.net/CTTestList1199.html

Fullan, Michael G. (1991) **The New Meaning of Educational Change.** New York: Teachers College Press.

Joyce, Bruce R. and Weil, Marsha. (1996) **Models of Teaching.** Needham Heights, MA: Allyn & Bacon.

Joyce, B. (Ed). (1990) **Changing School Culture through Staff Development.** Alexandria, VA: ASCD.

Lieberman, Ann and Miller, Lynne. (1999) **Teachers—Transforming Their World and Their Work.** New York: Teachers College Press.

Lieberman, A. (1995) **The Work of Restructuring Schools: Building from the Ground Up.** New York: Teachers College Press

McCombs, jennifer,. et. al. (2004) "Achieving State and National

References

Literacy Goals, a Long Uphill Road." The Rand Corporation. http://www.rand.org/publications/TR/TR180/

Melchior, Timothy M. "Counterpoint thinking: Connecting Learning and thinking in Schools." http://www.chss.montclair.edu/inquiry/spr95/melchior.html.

Melville, Herman. **Moby Dick**.

Miller, Debbie. (2002) **Reading With Meaning: Teaching Comprehension in the Primary Grades**. Stenhouse Publishers.

Oppenheimer, Todd. (2003) **The Flickering Mind: The False Promise of Technology in the Classroom and How Learning Can Be Saved**. Random House.

Postman, Neil and Weingartner, Charles. (1971) **Teaching As a Subversive Activity**. Delta.

Shenk, David. (1997) **Data Smog.** New York: Harper Edge.

Taba, Hilda. (1988) "A Conceptual Framework for Curriculum Design," **Curriculum: An Introduction to the Field**, ed. James R. Gress. Berkeley, CA: McCutchan Publishing Corporation, pp. 276-304.

von Oech, Roger. (1998) **A Whack on the Side of the Head**. U.S. Games Systems.

Appendix A - The Student QDP

1. I explore important questions and issues arising out of the content of this class.
never __ monthly__ weekly __ 2-3 times weekly __ daily __

2. My teacher challenges me to do my own thinking, build my own answers and interpret information independently.
never __ monthly__ weekly __ 2-3 times weekly __ daily __

3. I am expected to center my research around an essential question of some kind.
never __ monthly__ weekly __ 2-3 times weekly __ daily __

4. I organize my thinking using Inspiration™ and other software programs to make mind maps.
never __ monthly__ weekly __ 2-3 times weekly __ daily __

5. I organize my thinking using paper to draw mind maps or cluster diagrams.
never __ monthly__ weekly __ 2-3 times weekly __ daily __

6. I work in a group to solve problems, make decisions and explore challenging questions.
never __ monthly__ weekly __ 2-3 times weekly __ daily __

7. I have the writing skills I need to handle research challenges effectively and efficiently.
strongly agree __ agree__ disagree__ strongly disagree __

8. I am getting quite good at knowing what each of the question types can do for me and how to combine or orchestrate their use.
strongly agree __ agree__ disagree__ strongly disagree __

9. My teacher presents the class with a challenge or issue, points us to a large collection of relevant information resources and expects us to figure things out.
never __ monthly__ weekly __ 2-3 times weekly __ daily __

10. I am able to make an important contribution to the work of a team considering a curriculum challenge.
strongly agree __ agree__ disagree__ strongly disagree __

11. The work we do in class and the tasks we must perform are going to prepare me for my life as an adult - both as a worker and as a community member.
__ strongly agree __ agree__ disagree__ strongly disagree

The Student QDP

12. Many of the things we study seem boring and senseless to me.
__ strongly agree __ agree__ disagree__ strongly disagree

13. I am getting more skilled at generating my own questions and figuring out how to build my own answers.
__ strongly agree __ agree__ disagree__ strongly disagree

14. I just do not enjoy exploring complicated questions that prove frustrating and would much rather just be told what to do, where to find answers and how to wrap things up quickly.
__ strongly agree __ agree__ disagree__ strongly disagree

15. We devote too little time to important questions in this class and memorize too much information I do not care about.
strongly agree __ agree__ disagree__ strongly disagree

16. My teacher does a good job of helping me without doing too much for me.
strongly agree __ agree__ disagree__ strongly disagree __

17. I have the reading skills I need to handle research challenges effectively and efficiently.
strongly agree __ agree__ disagree__ strongly disagree __

18. I have the information finding skills I need to handle research challenges effectively and efficiently.
strongly agree __ agree__ disagree__ strongly disagree __

19. This year has really helped me to get in touch with my own sense of wonder about things in life.
strongly agree __ agree__ disagree__ strongly disagree __

Appendix B - The Teacher QDP

1. I ask students to explore important questions and issues arising out of the content of my class.

never __ monthly __ weekly __ 2-3 times weekly __ daily __

2. I challenge students to do their own thinking, build their own answers and interpret information.

never __ monthly __ weekly __ 2-3 times weekly __ daily __

3. I encourage students to center their research around an essential question of some kind..

never __ monthly __ weekly __ 2-3 times weekly __ daily __

4. I expect students to organize their thinking using Inspiration™ and other software programs to make mind maps.

never __ monthly __ weekly __ 2-3 times weekly __ daily __

5. I expect students to organize their thinking using paper to draw mind maps or cluster diagrams.

never __ monthly __ weekly __ 2-3 times weekly __ daily __

6. I ask students to work in groups to solve problems, make decisions and explore challenging questions.

never __ monthly __ weekly __ 2-3 times weekly __ daily __

7. I have become quite good at adding to my repertoire of classroom moves, tactics and strategies to promote student questioning and wondering.

strongly agree __ agree__ disagree__ strongly disagree __

8. I really don't have the time or energy to do much lesson or unit development aimed at promoting student questioning.

strongly agree __ agree__ disagree__ strongly disagree __

9. I take pleasure in learning new approaches alongside of my peers in ways that are informal, casual and low-key.

strongly agree __ agree__ disagree__ strongly disagree __

10. I would need some kind of packaged program to make sure

my students have good questioning experiences.

strongly agree __ agree__ disagree__ strongly disagree __

11. There is so much curriculum content to cover that I can rarely take the time to engage students in group investigations and problem solving.

strongly agree __ agree__ disagree__ strongly disagree __

12. I am getting quite good at diagnosing which students need which skills at which times by observing them as they conduct research and by asking them good questions about what they are doing.

strongly agree __ agree__ disagree__ strongly disagree __

13. If I run into in a new task requiring skills I do not already possess, I am quite good at teaching myself the new skills or finding someone to help me learn them.

strongly agree __ agree__ disagree__ strongly disagree __

14. The district offers me a wide and rich menu of learning opportunities in support of the questioning and research goals that allow me to match my preferred learning styles with the activities I select.

strongly agree __ agree__ disagree__ strongly disagree __

15. There is not enough time for me to figure out smart ways to engage my classes in doing lots of questioning and investigating.

strongly agree __ agree__ disagree__ strongly disagree ____

16. If I get stuck or frustrated with something new, I know whom to turn to if I want support and assistance.

strongly agree __ agree__ disagree__ strongly disagree __

17. I would do more with student questioning if it were not for the pressures that are loaded onto me by the new state standards and tests.

strongly agree __ agree__ disagree__ strongly disagree __

18. I am making more time now than I used to for students to do more of the thinking - analyzing, interpreting, inferring and synthesizing.

strongly agree __ agree__ disagree__ strongly disagree __

19. I spend lots of time wondering how I can make questioning and wondering a major focus in my classes.

strongly agree __ agree__ disagree__ strongly disagree __

Index

Index